Communicating
Effectively

SUSAN DELLINGER
BARBARA DEANE

Communicating Effectively

a complete guide for better managing

CHILTON BOOK COMPANY
Radnor, Pennsylvania

To Bob and Jade (for their love and support), and to my professors at the University of Colorado (for the theory) and my managers at GTE (for the practice).

Susan Dellinger

To my family and my students for making me learn to be a better communicator—thank you.

Barbara Deane

Published in Radnor, Pennsylvania, by Chilton Book Company and simultaneously in Don Mills, Ontario, Canada, by Thomas Nelson & Sons, Ltd.

Library of Congress Catalog Card No. 79-8393

ISBN 0-8019-6880-1
ISBN 0-8019-6881-x

Designed by Anne Churchman

Manufactured in the United States of America

1 2 3 4 5 6 7 8 9 0   9 8 7 6 5 4 3 2 1 0

Contents

Contents

Preface

This book is designed to help you communicate more effectively with the people you work with. Briefly, it will help you be a better manager.

As a manager, communicating well is one of your prime responsibilities. Today, business men and women are primarily concerned with managing people, and the higher you go in an organization, the better "people skills" and communications skills you will need. All those tasks you perform—departmental planning, implementation of those plans, budgeting, performance appraisal, motivating and organizing others, dealing with your customers, reporting to top management, running meetings—all depend upon your ability to think, to organize, and to *communicate.*

The skills needed to communicate well are learned just as tennis is learned: by getting out and practicing. Although "We need better communications" has become a business cliché, what is often meant by "better communications" is simply "more communicating," more swinging at the ball even though the stroke is hopeless in the belief that maybe, this time, the shot will go over the net.

All the practice in the world will do you no good if you practice the wrong things. Since most people have learned communications skills poorly, they habitually practice the wrong things, and they are not the superior managers they could be. Hence, this book.

Our emphasis is on the practical. Each chapter begins with a set of questions designed to show you what the chapter covers. As you read, you will discover skills you need to practice and the strategies to implement. You can immediately use what you have learned every day at work. (In addition to skills and strategies, we try to give you enough theory to understand *why* you're doing what you're doing.)

Exercises at the end of each chapter will help you build your skills in each area of communications. By doing the exercises, you will be able to discover how what you've learned in that chapter works for you. (Of course, you don't *have* to do them. You can skip over the exercises and go on reading. But we hope you'll be intrigued enough to try at least some of them.)

Communication is a very broad concept. We have attempted to cover the entire range of communication situations that you will encounter in business. For convenience in presenting a complicated subject, the book is divided into two parts: Receiving (listening) and Sending (speaking and writing), corresponding to the simultaneous roles of receiver and sender, audience and actor, that each of us plays as we interact with others on the job.

We hope that you will enjoy using this book as you learn from it. Just as a sport becomes more enjoyable as your skill increases, so communicating becomes more enjoyable as you get better at it.

This book should be of long-range as well as immediate benefit. You will probably want to return to it from time to time to review the material and re-do the exercises. Each time that you do, you will be a slightly different person, in different circumstances. Communicating well is not something you learn once and forget. It's an ongoing, dynamic process that you can begin working on at any age and at any stage of your career, and you can continue to improve as long as you live.

Communicating Effectively

1

The Business of Communicating

The advance of science has enabled man to
communicate at twice the speed of sound while
he still acts at half the speed of sense.

ANON.

PREVIEW

1. When you think of communicating, do you picture
yourself telling something to someone else? Are you most
often the initiator or the receiver of the communication?

2. Have you had a boss who was more interested in what
he or she had to say than in listening to others? How good a
boss was that person?

3. Do you sometimes find that your idea of what happened at a meeting is different from what others thought
happened?

4. Do you prefer to talk to a business associate face to
face or over the telephone? Why?

5. Do you feel that you are a better communicator one-
to-one than in front of a group? Why?

6. Do you feel that you can talk people into doing what
you want them to? Are you more or less effective than your
associates?

7. Do you usually plan what you intend to say before
you talk with someone? Does the discussion usually go according to your plan?

8. Have you ever heard some comment about yourself that you can't understand, such as you're "opinionated" or "unsociable" or "too easy going"? Do you know what you're doing and saying to give this impression?

9. Have you ever received a verbal message and had the feeling that the person meant more than he or she said? Do you follow up this intuition, or isn't it important?

George Gage, popular president of General Telephone of Florida, speaking to his middle managers, was asked to identify the largest problem in the company, as he viewed it, from the crow's nest. His answer: "Communication. Our people don't talk to each other."

When asked to elaborate, he explained: "If you and I exchange silver dollars, what will I end up with? One silver dollar. However, if you and I exchange ideas, what will I end up with? Two ideas—yours and mine." And perhaps a third or fourth idea that no one would have thought of alone—that is the kind of stimulation created by communication.

Humans communicate in order to gain something from another. It might be to gain important information or to understand another's viewpoint. But communication has a purpose, whether large or small, clear or fuzzy, conscious or unconscious. The most common reason for communication between manager and subordinate is to give and receive information. The traditional manager might see his role as limited to giving the information—orders, assignments, rules—and the subordinate's as restricted to acting on it. This limited view is typified by a remark made by the owner of a small business when we told him about this book. "What's all this junk about developing communication skills? You tell people what to do and, by God, they'd better do it!"

That approach might still be used in some businesses, but it's no longer very effective. No longer are people willing merely to be told what to do. They want a say in their work lives because their work is important to them. They feel that they deserve answers to their questions and reasons for the duties they are asked to perform. In order to perform well, they need to know how they contribute to the company's success—and that their contribution is encouraged and recognized. If you communicate only to give orders, then it is time to reexamine your management style and try new communications tools.

EXCHANGING IDEAS

It is not only reasonable, but invaluable, to communicate with a subordinate in order to *receive* information. Because the modern business organization is much too complex for one person to know everything firsthand, information must be obtained from others. In general, the more and better your information, the better your ideas will be. If you just give away your ideas you will eventually go broke. To stay solvent, you must learn to receive and value the ideas of others. Sometimes, ideas must be solicited; at other times, they will be offered freely. The important thing is to be *receptive* to them.

Unfortunately, many managers appear to value only the ideas of those who are above them on the corporate ladder. But where do the people at the top of the ladder get their ideas? After all, there's nobody above them. Usually, the people at the top realize that good ideas come from many sources, both above and below. Often, these people are superb *listeners*. Robert Woodruff of Coca-Cola, one of the outstanding business executives of the twentieth century, was known as a man who listened rather than talked. Whenever he had an important decision to make, he solicited information and opinions from a wide variety of people, including his chauffeur. In fact, whenever one of his company executives wanted to know if Mr. Woodruff was close to making a decision, he'd ask his chauffeur, "Has he asked you yet?" Important information and ideas are available almost everywhere in your organization—if you are open to them. An old axiom in corporate life says, "To get ahead, you need people pushing from below and pulling from above." Those people are more willing to "push" and "pull" if they have received useful information and ideas from you—and have been encouraged to give you information, too.

Some managers are receptive to the ideas of others but have a habit of hoarding those ideas to themselves. One manager we knew was expert at surrounding herself with people who had great new ideas, but she made two mistakes: when she passed on ideas, she claimed them as her own instead of crediting her co-workers; and, once she had drained people of their ideas, she withdrew her support. Her net gain was mostly hostility from her fellow workers. Her loss: she was a total failure in developing the people under her, an important managerial responsibility.

In order to learn from her mistakes, two important principles must be kept in mind. The first, when you receive information and ideas, give credit where credit is due. This is not a moral nicety, but a practical necessity. Otherwise, you destroy morale. The second is that, as a manager, you are responsible for the development of your subordinates' potential. It is hardly sound practice to "shed" people like yesterday's clothes, yet some companies and their executives use up people the way Henry VIII used up wives.

The companies and managers who do this (and it's usually obvious from the higher turnover figures) know very little about human beings. People are dynamic, capable of growing, and capable of constantly producing new ideas—*if* the climate is right. Those who generate new ideas know that the creative part of the brain is like a muscle: the more it's used, the stronger it becomes. If you, as a manager, encourage people to produce ideas and give them credit, they are going to produce more and better ideas. If you can make people feel valued, they will be challenged to do even better.

Here's how the manager can best benefit from the people who report to him:

1. The manager hires qualified, capable employees.
2. The manager develops an attitude of receptivity to people and really listens to them.

3. The manager both gives and receives information and ideas in order to stimulate and motivate employees.
4. The manager believes in their capabilities and potential and expresses that belief to them. He or she understands that it takes time and nurturing to produce maximum growth.
5. The manager treats people exactly as he or she would like to be treated. (This rule is still golden.)

Look at that list again. The manager selects, listens, is receptive, stimulates, motivates, believes, expresses, understands, treats—in a word, *communicates*.

PRINCIPLES OF COMMUNICATION

At this point let us look at several underlying principles of communication and some of the basic factors affecting every communication situation. This will provide a background for the skills described in subsequent chapters. Some of these principles are obvious; others are more complex. No doubt you are already aware of many of them, but everybody needs a refresher from time to time.

1. *Each communication situation is unique.* When we communicate, we are involved in a dynamic process involving movement and responses that occur in a special order. Certain words will be chosen, certain movements of the body will be made which are particularly suited for that moment and which make the situation a vital happening, unfolding moment by moment.

Since no two situations are alike, there can be no fixed rules about how to communicate. Behavior will vary according to the people and the situation. Basic *principles*, however, can be adapted to fit each circumstance. This requires intelligence and thought, because sometimes you have to break old, conditioned responses in order to develop a repertoire of strategies that can be at your command for each situation.

2. *The key to successful communication is FEED-BACK.* Without receiving feedback from the people you communicate with, you will never know whether you are getting your message across. At one conference on communication for managers, all who attended were later asked by the conference organizers for their evaluation of the keynote address. They agreed that the speaker was brilliant, an expert in his field, that his presentation of facts and theory was flawless, but that the address was not relevant to their work. They had no idea how it applied to their situation because it was not in language that "spoke to their condition," as the Quakers say. Thus it was a failure.

This happens all too frequently—the sender does not ask for feedback, and the receiver gives none or gives inaccurate feedback (for fear of offending, perhaps). The sender continues with his off-target messages in blissful ignorance, like a vending machine that dispenses soft drinks into the drain because it doesn't know it's out of cups.

How could the speaker have found out that he was not getting his message across in time to do something about it? Simply by asking. During the course of his presentation, he could have solicited feedback that would help him gear his message to his audience. Or, after the conference, the evaluation results would show him that he had missed his target, and he might be able to change his approach next time.

If you are the receiver, it is your responsibility to give accurate feedback information to the sender so he or she knows that you understand the message. As a sender, it's your job to elicit feedback, to note your listeners' responses and ask questions.

3. *Face-to-face communication is the most effective.* With today's sophisticated communications systems—telephones, radios, films, television, satellite stations—why do we still pay large amounts of money to fly in a guest speaker for a conference. Why does one executive get on a plane in Seattle while another gets on a plane in New York so that they can meet in Chicago for a two-hour conference?

Simply because there is no substitute for face-to-face communication. It still conveys the most information, and it affords immediate verbal and visual feedback.

When the receiver is not in front of you, it is more difficult to obtain feedback. The manager who relies heavily on memos, letters, and other written communications is cheating himself of the benefit of immediate verbal and visual response. Often the response never comes or it comes too late to be of use. This disadvantage must be weighed carefully before you choose written over face-to-face communication.

4. *Distractions can garble your message.*   Either the receiver or the sender can become distracted during the communication process and miss the message. For example, other people talking, nearby activity interruptions in the office, technical difficulties, illegible handwriting, are all "noise" that may jeopardize successful communication. Either the distraction seems to be more interesting than the message, or the audience has so much difficulty concentrating on the message that they give up.

The manager should attempt to control any distractions by asking the secretary to hold phone calls or by going to a quiet conference room, for example. Not every distraction can be controlled, however. In addition to the annoying noises outside, people can also be distracted by "inner noises"—their own tensions, anxieties, and worries. Indeed, anxiety was once defined by a psychologist as the habit of paying more attention to one's inner feelings than to the task at hand. In this case, communication with the outside world invariably suffers.

5. *The more people who are involved, the more complex communication becomes.*   Many managers are better communicating one-on-one than at a meeting or in groups. In fact, most people do prefer a one-on-one situation because it's much easier to deal with. Each time another person joins the communications process, problems of sending and receiving, understanding, interpreting feedback, overcoming distractions, and so on are multiplied. That is why,

although executives hold a number of meetings during a typical workweek, the real decision-making often takes place in private one-on-one conferences, behind closed doors. The more receivers you have, the harder it is to tailor your message for each one. At the same time, it is more difficult for each receiver to provide you the necessary feedback. The larger the number of receivers, the lower the probability of accurate interpretations.

6. *Every message contains both information and emotions.* While you are delivering a verbal message, even in the most carefully chosen, "objective" language, you are also conveying your feelings by means of voice inflection, facial expression, body posture, and other nonverbal behavior. The words themselves connote feelings, and a word considered neutral to the sender may be emotionally laden to the receiver.

People operate at a *cognitive* (objective, informational) level and an *affective* (subjective, emotional) level simultaneously. In every message, either the cognitive or the emotional content will be stronger. This is not a problem unless they contradict each other and convey two different messages.

Many managers seem unaware of the messages about feelings that they both send and receive. For example, if you tell someone to implement a new policy, but your tone of voice says, "I know it's going to be a nuisance, and it isn't really that important," don't be surprised when nothing gets done.

If you are the receiver, and a person's words say one thing and tone of voice or body language says another, which is the true message and which should you pay more attention to? The skillful manager will determine the stronger message and "tune in," giving feedback accordingly. This may mean losing some of the words in order to be more attentive to body language or tone of voice, or concentrating on the words rather than on nonverbal behavior.

7. *Words are symbols used to express thoughts, and they are always open to interpretation.* Language is a coding

system which, like Morse Code or semaphore signals, has *no meaning* other than what the communicators assign to it by mutual agreement. Therefore, it is crucial that both sender and receiver attach the same meaning to the symbol.

Too often, managers think that their meanings will be clear to others. But if I am told that I am "seriously behind in my work," does that mean that I am two days, two weeks, or two months behind, or that the work itself is substandard? I may choose from any of these alternatives, and more, because the symbols have not been specific enough to express the thought.

Communication is also more difficult among diverse peoples. Understanding is easier when people in an organization speak the same language. "No one said anything aloud," says a physician with working-class background in Doris Lessing's *The Golden Notebook*. "But the upper middle classes communicate with each other in inaudible squeaks, like bats. It puts people of my background at a terrible disadvantage."

Indeed, the more homogeneous the group, the less effort it takes to communicate. Homogeneity may, however, rapidly be becoming the exception rather than the rule. As more minorities and women enter the managerial ranks, assuming that "everybody knows what I mean" is more and more risky. Communicating well with a diverse group has become more important than ever before.

8. *Selective perception can distort the message.*   Rarely do any two people observe an event, evaluate it, and act on it in the same way. Ten people who witness an automobile accident will give ten different versions of what happened. Similarly, the same information given to ten people at a meeting will result in ten different interpretations. Fortunately, there is usually enough overlap so that each gets the major part of the message.

These differences in interpretation are caused by *selective perception,* each person's brain selecting from multiple stimuli the ones that seem most important. The classic case of selective perception is the amateur photographer who focuses only on the adorable child and snaps the picture. But when the print comes back, there's a telephone pole growing out of the child's head. Where did that come from? It was there all along, of course, but the photographer, concentrating only on his subject, didn't see it. In listening to any message, people will choose what is most interesting or relevant to them, and that is what they will remember. If this is not what the sender wanted them to remember, communication has failed.

While selective perception can be a problem, the manager can also benefit from it. The key is to value individual differences, and, in fact, to encourage them. Because people do perceive things differently, it follows that, if encouraged, they will provide multiple solutions to a problem.

9. *People communicate according to their expectations of a situation.* Problems arise if one's expectations about a communication situation are different from reality or from others' expectations. We plan our behavior, as well as our dress, actions, and language, according to our expectations. If we find that the actual situation is different, we may continue to do the wrong thing or attempt to adjust. Although it's never wise to preplan and rehearse every word, it is always wise to check to see if others' expectations match yours or clarify expectations before pursuing a discussion. The following story is a case study of the pitfalls of unclarified expectations:

Henry "Hank" Ward had been vice-president of operations for only two months. His upward movement in the company had been quick and sure. He started as a line manager eight years ago and was a vice-president at thirty-nine. His last two months had been a test of his mettle, but he seemed to have an ability to size up and respond to a situation quickly, and he emerged from each bout unscathed.

Before he left for a meeting at corporate headquarters in New York, he hadn't been clear on why the president had asked him to attend. But it was too late to worry about it. Probably just another "Let's check out the new man" session. When Hank appeared at the conference center for the 7 A.M. meeting, he noticed that he was the only vice-president of operations present. Most of the other executives were either marketing men or company presidents. He thought this was a bit odd but assumed he was merely representing the Midwest company and that someone at home base would interpret the information he brought back. So he relaxed, took occasional notes, and listened to the chairman drone.

Three hours later, the chairman called a fifteen-minute break. Everyone left except Hank and the chairman, who promptly asked Hank's opinion on every detail. Suddenly, the light dawned. The meeting was really for him, Hank Ward. He was now viewed as the "expert" in strategic planning, and the marketing people needed his approval before Corporate would accept their proposal. Quickly his mind raced back over the past three hours to try to recapture the main points of the meeting well enough to make intelligent comments.

Hank pulled out all right. He managed to persuade the group to summarize their conclusions, and he actively participated during the rest of the day. However, some extremely awkward moments could have been prevented if he'd taken the time to check out his expectations about the meeting's purpose and his role in it.

The moral of this story is that expectations should be aired early so that everyone is aware of them. Otherwise, each person will be playing under a different set of rules. It is never safe to assume that everyone shares your unspoken expectations.

10. *If they don't trust you, they won't understand you.* Management often has the naive idea that "all we need is more communication." However, if no firm foundation of trust exists within an organization, increased communication will make things worse, not better. Since communications received in an atmosphere of distrust and suspicion will be misinterpreted, they will succeed only in fouling things up further.

Every manager should find this to be self-evident, but that is not always the case. Whether by accident or by design, some managers seem to thrive on misunderstanding.

When a manager unknowingly causes misunderstanding, confusion, and mistrust, he needs to improve his communications skills. When he knowingly causes misunderstanding, he is either very insecure or he is keeping power and control in his hands by pitting one executive against another. But such Byzantine empires eventually break up and, while they last, they're not very pleasant places in which to live.

On the other hand, if you create an atmosphere of trust, you will more likely find out what's really going on rather than what people think you want to hear. People who report to you need to feel that you will be fair enough to hear their side of the story and secure enough to listen to their honest disagreements or unpleasant news. If you have the maturity and inner security to encourage fruitful, honest communication, you will succeed in creating understanding and a productive work environment.

EXERCISES

1. In one work day, keep a chart recording the people you gave information to and the people you received information from. See if you are basically a sender or a receiver of information. To or from whom? Under what circumstances?

2. On the same chart, add a category for *cognitive* and *affective* information. Try to determine if the information given or received was mainly about factual, objective matters or about feelings. Which kind are you getting and giving to which sources? Do certain people provide you with information on feelings and others with more factual data? Do you, in turn, select certain people to communicate with about facts and others feelings? Try to figure out why.

3. At the next meeting you attend, make a list of the things you are paying attention to at any given moment. About every five minutes, write down the item, person, or action that you are paying attention to. What kinds of things or behaviors are distracting? See if any pattern emerges.

4. After the meeting is over, question at least three other participants about the main points of the meeting. Look for similarities and differences of perception and opinions. Try to decide what caused these differences. If you were in charge of the meeting, ask at least three people to summarize the main points (in writing, so they can't change their minds under the influence of others' perceptions).

5. Choose a communications situation (interview, meeting, discussion) to analyze. Before it happens, write down your expectations about the situation. After it's over, look at what you wrote and see how accurate your prediction was.

6. As you review your "expectation list," ask yourself if you did anything in the situation to fulfill your expectations. If so, what? Did someone else seem to have different expectations? If so, how were the differences resolved?

7. When the next person comes in to talk with you, use a new word in your conversation. Choose an unusual word whose meaning you don't think this person will know. See if you're asked for a definition or whether the person chooses to interpret the symbol in his or her way or to misunderstand.

8. Purposefully start a discussion with someone and see if you can persuade that person to your point of view. Just for the practice, play devil's advocate and choose a point of view that you don't really believe and that is not characteristic of you. If you succeed in convincing this person, ask him or her what it was that you said or did that convinced them.

9. The next time that someone comes in your office unannounced, stop what you're doing and carry on a conversation of at least twenty minutes. While you are in conversation, make a mental list of all the times you're interrupted and the nature of the interruptions. If there are many, decide what you can do about preventing them.

10. For the next week, instead of using the telephone for interoffice calls, go see the person instead. Determine if you are more or less satisfied with the way the situation was handled in person rather than by telephone. At the end of the week, make a list of the types of situations that you feel

are best handled by phone and those that are better handled with face-to-face communication. Try to stick to your list.

11. Whenever you have a face-to-face conversation during the next week, use words you know the person will understand and then ask for feedback. Does he or she agree? What does he/she think?

2

Communicating with Yourself

We have met the enemy and he is us.

POGO

PREVIEW

1. During conversations, do you sometimes wonder what the other person is thinking about you: Does he or she like you? think you are smart? find you attractive?

2. Do you sometimes say things you later regret? Or are you reticent and later wish that you'd spoken up?

3. Who are the people you spend time with on a daily basis? Are they analytical and interested in self-improvement? Do you find them boring, stimulating, or neutral?

4. What are you reading? Watching on television? Seeing at the movies? Can you identify a pattern in the types of things you read about and watch? Do you actively select what you read or see or just follow old habits?

5. Do you sometimes feel that people at work don't understand you or appreciate you? Have you tried to figure out why?

6. Have you considered going back to school recently—college courses at night, a workshop, a management devel-

opment seminar? What subject or subjects are you interested in studying?

In this chapter we are temporarily turning our backs on others in order to concentrate on communicating with yourself. This may seem totally irrelevent at the moment, and you may be tempted to skip over this chapter. Please don't. Communicating honestly with yourself is an important first step—the foundation, in fact—of communicating with others. To communicate with the outer world effectively, you have to begin at the beginning—"in here," within yourself.

If you want to improve the communications environment at work, you can try to change other people, or you can try to change yourself. Often, it's easier and simpler to change yourself first. By changing yourself, you will inevitably effect changes in other people as they respond to restore the balance of the interactional equation.

This chapter is about improving intrapersonal communication, about improving your dialogue with yourself, your ability to recognize and explore your feelings, needs, and capabilities. What you learn here will pay off in spades when it comes time to communicate with others. The more self-knowledge you possess, the more self-confidence and ability you will have to present yourself favorably and positively to others.

LISTENING TO YOUR INNER VOICE

Everyone has an inner voice that they listen to with varying degrees of attentiveness. Psychologists tell us that we constantly talk to ourselves, consciously or unconsciously. Sometimes we are self-denigrating ("Look at what you just did! Why don't you do it right the first time!") or anxious ("I wonder if I should have said that—what must he think of me?") But internal dialogue needn't be negative. Negative feelings can be transformed into positive encouragement ("Well, I goofed up running that meeting, but I learned what not to do. The next one is going to be better."), or into a kind of internal cheerleading ("You can do it!"), a method used by many athletes.

Often, we fail to recognize and articulate our internal thoughts or feelings and instead experience vague feelings of dissatisfaction, boredom, anxiety. However, those unexpressed feelings may indicate problems, solutions, or courses of action that are worth pursuing. Pressures of business life and stress in other areas can lead to the uneasy feeling of being "out of sync." Taking stock more frequently in order to get in touch with where we are in relation to our surroundings can help to reduce anxiety about change and lead to a healthy way of coping.

Daydreams and Fantasies

Daydreaming is one of our more interesting forms of intrapersonal communication. You are fully conscious but far removed from the normal flow of events. You may find yourself staring blankly at the same worksheet that's been lying on your desk for an hour. Where did the time go? You have no idea—your body was present but your mind was out to lunch.

Fantasizing is a form of daydreaming that has a "wishing" dimension. Fantasies are usually dramatic in nature and involve actions that one would rarely, if ever, perform in reality. Fantasizing, like daydreaming, has traditionally been frowned upon by our practical-minded society. What could be more unbusinesslike or a bigger waste of time? However, fantasies do serve a useful purpose in the human personality. "Imagination is the will of things," wrote poet Wallace Stevens, meaning that we can will to accomplish only what we can first imagine. Psychologists have begun to view fantasizing in a new light. Often, the fantasy contains some kernel of truth about a person, if only he or she can come to recognize it.

Fantasies also enable us to "try out" new experiences first before we risk them in real life. For example, if you are thinking of changing jobs, you can fantasize about yourself playing this new role: how you would look and act, how others would react to you, what you would say to them. Similarly, imagining in advance an awkward situation may provide you with the courage to perform better when the situation arrives. The actual thing will seem like a reenactment of something you've already handled.

Some top executives, trial judges, and other decision makers use a technique that calls for this type of imagining. They visualize different alternatives, mull them over, and act them out in their minds. Then they play each one over like a film, comparing each solution. They ask themselves questions about each solution, store their feelings, perhaps give each solution some kind of score, then go on to the next.

A variant of this technique has been cited by a writer who interviewed a number of successful business people who were known for their "luck." One of the common traits was, surprisingly, pessimism. Each had the habit of imagining the worst thing that could possibly happen—and then preparing for it. Unlike the majority of people who would be inhibited from acting if they thought the worst might happen, these successful people went ahead with their plans, but they always had an escape route mapped out "in case." Imagining a number of different scenarios when working out plans can help prevent the type of rigid thinking that leads some managers to plunge blindly on a course of action like lemmings going over the legendary cliff.

Your daydreams and fantasies can also reflect a very real anxiety or frustration. You may not consciously recognize that a problem exists, but your unconscious may have become involved in trying to deal with it. If you can learn to acknowledge and utilize your fantasies and daydreams, you can often enlist the unconscious mind to help solve the problem.

"Sleep on It"

If you have ever been advised to sleep on something that was worrying you, you were being advised to turn the problem over to the unconscious mind. Many people say that they sleep on a problem or just forget about it for awhile and later the solution "just seems to come to them" out of the blue. Given time and space in which to work, the unconscious juggled the pieces until they fell into place, and then the solution appeared.

Dreaming is another form of intrapersonal communication. Although dream sequences often appear to be random and often quite absurd, with unusual combinations of people, places and events, an underlying problem or desire may be implicit in them. If you can learn to "listen in" on this form of internal dialogue, you may be able either to discover what's bothering you or to find a solution to some already identified problem. By remembering your dreams, by looking for repetitive patterns and analyzing them, it is possible to come to a better understanding of yourself. What are my fears and frustrations? Are they imaginary, or based on something in the real world I should take care of?

A young M.B.A. entered the family business and for the first few years, all seemed well—on the surface. But his father, who ran the company, refused to give him any raises and constantly undermined his decisions. Although only twenty-eight, the son already had an ulcer. He also had a recurrent dream that he was in a concentration camp. Occasionally, he was able to break out, but a rich family that lived in a castle on the hill overlooking the camp would capture him and drive him back into the prison. It doesn't take a trained psychiatrist to see that the "rich family on the hill" is the young businessman's own family. He quit the family business, got a new job with a national corporation and his ulcer healed. This admittedly is an extreme example, but what is your inner voice telling *you?*

CREATIVE THINKING

As we saw above, dreams, daydreams, and fantasies can aid our thinking and problem-solving abilities. By "thinking," we usually mean "critical thinking," the collection and sifting of facts, the analysis of data, use of logic, etc. But when it comes to problem solving, critical thinking is only half the story. Creative or "divergent" thinking does not follow habitual patterns of thought but makes its own pathways. Creative thinking utilizes material from both the unconscious and conscious mind. In fact, by depending only upon our critical faculties to analyze or solve a problem, we are probably trying to get along on half a brain. Recent research in how the brain works bears this out.

One of the more fascinating notions to emerge from recent studies of the functions of the brain is that of hemispheric (or cerebral) symmetry. There are two brain hemispheres, right and left. The left side is mainly devoted to analytic and logical processes, which are involved in such activities as mathematics, language, and deductive reasoning. The right side is devoted to the more creative, emotive, divergent mental functions, such as emotional expression, fantasy, and artistic expression.

The activities of the right hemisphere contribute considerably to the healthy functioning of the left. But, we tend to place such great value on logical thought that the left hemisphere gets all the exercise. If the right hemisphere is not used and stimulated, the person may lack imagination, be too highly structured, and his problem-solving abilities may be impaired. Even his logical thinking may not be as highly developed as when both hemispheres are working together.

Dreams, daydreams, and fantasies are related to right hemispheric functioning. Often they seem illogical, even "crazy," but they provide opportunities for us to utilize the creative side of the brain. Think again about that problem you were advised to sleep on. It is highly likely that during your waking hours, you worried at it with the logical part of the brain, analyzing and overanalyzing until a solution was completely obscured. However, if you dream about it and give it over to the right hemisphere, the creative side of the brain may provide the solution you're looking for.

The manager who seeks more creative solutions to problems or who feels he or she may be getting stale on the job and would like to tackle work in new ways can do several things.

First, you might divide your work functions according to those requiring logical analysis and those requiring more creativity. Of the typical managerial functions, those stimulating the left side of the brain would include routine tasks or those performed according to a predetermined system ("by the book"). Some left hemisphere functions would include short range planning (daily and weekly routine activities); scheduling (systematic approach to job assignments); organizing of materials and work load; routine reports; controlling (systematic measures of quality and quantity of production); and budgeting (allocating funds based on forecasted requirements). A manager who has a strong left-hemisphere orientation would be well suited to these types of functions. A "by the book" man is generally a strong left-sider: logical, systematic, methodical.

The right hemispheric functions are more difficult to define and often more difficult to perform.

A list of typical managerial functions requiring right hemisphere input might include employee counseling; interviewing and hiring; performance appraisal; organizing people; long-range planning and special project planning; zero-based budgeting; motivating others; delegating work and authority; disciplinary action and firing. Most of these functions require direct interaction with people; some, such as long-range planning and zero-based budgeting, involve unknown factors. For them, there is no set formula and certainly no fool-proof system. Thus these managerial functions need large applications of creative thought. These functions are the job responsibilities that you will not find all neatly tied up in a ready-to-use package in the policy manual.

EXPANDING THE RANGE OF YOUR INNER VOICE

All interpersonal exchanges must begin with intrapersonal content, and this content has to come from some-

where. You must have "input," as they say. If you are surrounded by negative people, don't be surprised if you, too,
feel negative. If you watch nothing on television but violent
crime programs, don't be surprised if, over a period of time,
you tend to feel a little edgy. Your mind is programmed by
whatever you or the world "out there" puts into it. You can
choose what will go in or, by not choosing, you can surren-
der the decisions to others—mass media, advertisers, the
"majority." If their choices are garbage, well—garbage in,
garbage out, as the computer saying goes.

Similarly, if you associate only with people who think,
act, dress and talk like you do, read only the same books or
watch only a narrow range of TV programs, where will any
new input come from? Your mind remains unstimulated,
locked into a closed system with no lines that open outside.
If this is your situation, take matters into your own hands.
Since you locked yourself in there, it follows that you can
also let yourself out. You alone control the key.

Sometimes, courage is needed to break out of the safety
of old patterns and expand your thinking. Some areas
within you may be painful or disturbing to face, but it's
necessary to do so if you want to change and improve. It
takes courage to expose your thoughts and feelings to yourself and others. Recognizing and listening to your inner
voice, and expanding its range can help you gain the insight necessary to turn outward and interact effectively
with others.

EXERCISES

1. Set your alarm fifteen minutes earlier in the morning.
If you are dreaming when the alarm goes off, try to drift
back to sleep to complete your dream. When you get up,
immediately write down what you remember about the
dream. Do this two or three times a week and see if a pattern emerges. If no meanings are clear, tell your dream to

another person. Sometimes, when telling another, a meaning will suddenly appear out of the blue.

2. The next time your mind wanders when you are doing solitary work in the office, let it wander. Build a fantasy around the subject of your thoughts. Then write it all down. Wait a few days or a week and read it over. Analyze it. Does it describe something you really want to do? Why haven't you done it?

3. If you have at least a fifteen-minute one-way commuting time alone, try to relax and let your mind wander aimlessly. Every time you find yourself thinking about a new subject, write it down in a notebook that you carry for that purpose. If you are driving, record your thoughts on a pocket tape recorder. See if any patterns emerge.

4. The next time that a sticky situation arises at the office, one without easy answers, try to solve it by involving your right hemisphere. Apply your usual logic to it, then try to forget about it for a couple of days and nights. Do any solutions come to you? If not, try to place the same problem in a different context. Mentally picture the people acting out various solutions.

5. The next time you wish you had spoken but didn't, write down what you were going to say. What might have happened if you'd said this? Try imagining the whole scene. Now try to imagine different possible reactions. See how many different scenarios you can come up with for the same situation.

6. Each time you attend a long meeting, place a stroke on a piece of scratch paper for every time your mind wanders. Do this again the following week, but write down what you were thinking about.

7. Complete the following open-ended sentences:
  I am happiest when I _____ .
  My greatest strength as a person is _____ .
  My greatest weakness is _____ .
  The accomplishment I am most proud of is _____ .
  The experience in my life I would most not like to
    repeat is _____ .

The part of my job I enjoy most is _____ .
The thing I wish I could change about my present
    job is _____.

Put the answers aside for at least a week, then take them
out and look at them. Any surprising answers? Try to analyze them and ask yourself why you think you responded as
you did.

3

The "Real You" and Your Business Image

O wad some power the giftie gie us
to see oursels as others see us!

ROBERT BURNS

PREVIEW

1. Are you concerned about your "image?" Do you know what image you have in the office?

2. Do you feel that you're better or worse—or different—than the image other people have of you? Do you want to do something about it?

3. When did you last feel that you were not a part of a group? What was the cause? Were you dressed differently? Was everybody else older, younger, of the opposite sex? Did the others share some interest you knew nothing about?

4. Are there certain types of people you feel uncomfortable around and can't communicate with (ethnic groups, men, women, certain personality types)? Do you want to try to communicate with them?

5. Do you find yourself playing certain stereotyped roles with other persons at work, such as Father Confessor, Big Brother, or Martyr? Did you choose your role or was it forced on you? Have you ever thought about changing it?

25

Once you begin to know yourself, you must learn to communicate that self to the outside world. The dilemma is how to reconcile the "real you" with the image or expectations that others have of you. When we communicate to others, we communicate not only what we think and feel, but also what kind of a person we are, and what they can expect from us. But what and how we communicate is governed not only by what kind of person we are "inside," but also by the demands of the role we are filling and the expectations of our audience.

THE BUSINESS IMAGE

Social roles play a tremendous part in communications. In many ways, they are convenient vehicles, facilitating communication. In other ways, the roles we unconsciously assume can interfere with getting our real messages through. Examples of social roles are parent/child, student/teacher, and various vocational roles: police officer, sales representative, airline pilot, corporation vice-president. Some roles are ascribed to us, while others, such as vocational roles, are deliberate choices.

With each role, however, come unwritten rules for behavior. From observation, from hints dropped by coworkers, from verbal and nonverbal clues, the individual learns how he is supposed to behave. Some stereotyping is inevitable, because the unwritten rules of the role are enforced by group consensus—by the audience.

Consider, for example, the role of the business executive. Does a picture of a white male in a conservative business suit come to mind? This image has resulted from generations of middle-class white males playing the role, and such a person should be able to step right into it fairly easily.

Within the past generation, however, society has changed the rules. Women and minorities are now supposed to play the role too. But the stereotyped image changes slowly. Thus role behavior that is second nature to white males requires some real effort and agonizing by new players of the game. How is a woman to dress for a career in management, for example, when she has little idea of what her audience expects a woman manager to look like? What if the new role behavior conflicts with her earlier conditioning in how to play the social role of "woman"? If you're black, should you give up your "natural" hair style to conform to a white audience's preferences? Should someone tone down exuberant gestures in order to be more in line with the majority's behavior? Should you work with a speech teacher to rid yourself of a West Texas twang?

Assuming new roles, changing the "outside" without also making changes on the inside, can be difficult and even painful. A social role is an integral part of one's personality. Ethnic identity, for example, is intertwined with personal identity, and changing to conform to another image may be more of a sacrifice than you're willing or able to make. On the other hand, a social role may become so ingrained that an individual is unaware of it. The role becomes one's identity, so to speak, and some executives find that they have retired from their identities along with their jobs.

Occasionally, people change inside and the role that formerly fit well is now too confining. If the role cannot be expanded or changed, the individual may shed it as a snake sheds its skin and change careers in mid-life. Sometimes an individual from the "correct" background for a role—who should fit right into it—doesn't. One thirtyish man we know, who began a career as a banker in line with family expectations, hated wearing a suit and being confined to an office. He traded his business suit for a pair of jeans and now runs a chain of country barbecue stands, which is more in line with the "real person" he feels that he is.

LIFE SCRIPTS

Another type of role that psychologists have recognized recently has more to do with one's early socialization within the family. Transactional analysis and "script" anal-

ysis have made us aware of multiple "voices in the head"
and the part played by families in casting children in certain roles. Transactional analysis describes three "people"
that we have in our heads at all times: our Child, who gets
us into trouble but who is also the creative, spontaneous
part of our personalities; our Adult, who is rational but not
always in control; and our Parent, the internalized voices of
our parents who still sometimes tell us what to do.

The late Dr. Eric Berne in his bestselling *Games People
Play* described some of the neurotic "life scripts" that
people act out instead of responding rationally to life as it
really is, here and now. Everyone plays these games to a
certain extent. Indeed, our responses to others on the job
are frequently distorted by game playing. These theories
also give us new insight into the "inner voice" discussed in
Chapter 2. You need to know which voice is speaking when
you tune in on yourself intrapersonally. Our Adult may say,
"Hold your temper; you'll say something that you'll regret
later," while our Child says, "Who does he think he is,
anyway? Tell him off!" Which one do we listen to?

Instead of reacting realistically to other people at work,
we sometimes cast them into roles that fit our own script
needs. The result is very distorted communication indeed.
It's possible not only to watch some of these games in action
where you work, but also to catch yourself at it once in a
while.

One life script is the Damsel in Distress. She can perform
routine aspects of her job, but if any tough decisions come
along, she's conditioned to look for a Knight to slay her
dragons. Since many men have Dragon Slayer scripts (particularly in the middle-aged and older generations),
Knights are usually not difficult to find. If this woman is
career-minded, however, she's in for a lot of disappointment, since Knights get promoted, but Damsels in Distress
rarely do.

One woman we know began her academic career with a
job in a midwestern university in which she was the only
woman among twenty-five males in the math department.
The department was badly managed by its chairman and

riddled with strife and jealousy. She wrote, "I found my-
self, day after day, listening to my male colleagues as they
came to me, one by one, to pour out their frustrations and
complaints. They did it as if it were their right, as if I had
no problems of my own."

Not an unusual situation. Men in a business setting frequently will not confide in other males but will to a woman
because they've been conditioned to think of women as
natural confidantes, not as competitors. However, in this
case, the woman colluded with them. By listening pa-
tiently, she signaled her willingness to play Den Mother to
their Cub Scouts.

Even if people are not under the unconscious control of a
script, they may be carrying around unconscious instructions from a Parent figure which are totally inappropriate to
their present situation. One young executive sought counseling because he suffered from insomnia. He would lie
awake at night, reliving the events of the day and totaling
up his accumulations of hurts and angers. Therapy revealed that this was a "script" directive from his mother:
"Notice every negative thing so that you can feel hurt."

A young woman management trainee was driving her
male supervisor wild by refusing to express her own judgments. Whenever a problem arose, she would try to manipulate him into giving her the answer, obviously still acting
under a parental directive that it was inappropriate to form
or express her own opinions. She was supposed to let men
make the decisions—or at least, think that they had. But this
unconscious directive was jeopardizing her job perfor
mance and her position in the management training
program.

A department manager tried to hold meetings once a
month that were supposed to be completely "open";
everybody in the department was supposedly free to express an opinion. However, the manager always held back
important information. He would allow someone to speak
up and then zap them with some piece of information that
proved them wrong. (Berne called this game, "Now I've
got you, you son-of-a-bitch!" The manager's father might

have played it with him when he was a boy. Parents frequently play it with children and teachers with students.) The people in the department soon became so gun-shy that they practically refused to open their mouths at these meetings. The manager has heard complaints that the meetings are dull and unproductive, and he can't figure out why.

As these examples show, often the internal, intrapersonal communication operates powerfully but unconsciously. We simply are not aware of the signals we're sending and the ways in which we are influencing other people's behavior. Sometimes, feedback from friends and co-workers or counseling will reveal the problem (the sleepless executive, as soon as a psychologist pointed out his mother's role in his behavior, was able to turn her off at night and go to sleep). And if you understand the game, you can refuse to play it. For instance, if the professor had stopped listening, her male colleagues would have found somebody else to fill her Mother role and begun treating her like a colleague.

ASSUMING NEW ROLES

Role discomfort is usually most acute in people entering a new vocation or in people promoted or transferred into a new job. The individual may sometimes feel like a fraud, a "con man" who may be exposed at any moment. He thinks, "Is this the way a vice-president is supposed to behave?" and "If I do or say this, will they think I don't really belong in this job?" This kind of anxiety is inevitable at first, for a person's credibility in a role is judged according to the audience's expectations. The role player has to look and act the part in order to be accepted by the audience. Under these conditions, subordinates can produce as much anxiety in the new vice-president as the boss produces in the new trainee.

Usually, these anxieties fade in time. When they are excessive or when they persist, however, the individual may be so insecure that he may put others down in order to build himself up, or act overbearing and tyrannical, "overacting" in order to convince others and himself that he really is what he is supposed to be. Sometimes, an individual may feel that his entire existence is just a set of responses to "outside" expectations, a machine programmed to respond. Spontaneity in communicating with others becomes impossible. He or she either calculates every utterance in order not to endanger his or her image or reacts mechanically to everything.

This does not have to happen, of course. Ideally, as a person becomes more comfortable in his or her new role, "inside" and "outside," the "real you" and the requirements of your role strike a balance. Individual personality is able to modify the role and the expectations of the audience as well. Also, the amount of conformity to the businessperson image will vary greatly from one organization to another and even among departments within the same organization. In some companies, the creative types in the advertising department look and act differently from other employees; in other companies, it's the computer department that's different.

How much do the managers and executives in your company resemble each other? How much room is there for individual style and personality? Do you feel that you can adapt your own personality to the demands of your role in this particular company? The answers to these intrapersonal questions will affect your ability to communicate within that company. (More on analyzing the organization's style and your part in it in Chapter 8.)

EXERCISES

1. Divide your co-workers into those who seem to fit well into their roles and those who don't. Analyze the difference between them. Consider physical appearance (height, weight, hairstyle, grooming, clothing), mannerisms, poise, posture. Now analyze yourself in terms of your work role. Any changes needed? What will you do about them?

2. The next time you are in a group of people and feel uncomfortable with them, take a passive role in the group and analyze what is making you feel uncomfortable. Consider things like age, dress, sex, language, methods of expression, etc. Are certain people dominators? Do they expect you to lead them and does it make you uncomfortable? Once you've identified some actual causes of your discomfort, see if some of them can be safely ignored, and if others can be positively adapted to.

3. Find someone at work who often seems to make you play a specific role when you are around him (son/daughter, father/mother). The next time this happens, analyze what specific communication behaviors this person uses to call up this role in you. See if you can prevent this from happening and be your own, adult self in this interaction.

4. For the next month, every time someone gives you information about yourself, write it down. Try not to seek it out, but don't discourage it either. See if you learn anything about yourself that you didn't know before.

5. Pretend that you are about to retire. Give yourself an award. What would you like it to say? What do you think it *will* say?

4

Why Don't People Listen Around Here?

God gave us two ears and one tongue so that
we could listen twice as much as we talk.

FOLK SAYING

PREVIEW

1. Do you think of yourself as a good listener? What evidence do you have to support your opinion?

2. Think of the two best listeners you know. What do they do that others do not? How can you prove that they are good listeners?

3. Think of situations in which you tend to "turn off" your listening. Why do you do this in this particular situation?

4. When you find yourself in a stressful situation (e.g., with an important client) are you really listening to the other person or do you become more concerned with what you will say?

5. Do you often just seem to "know" what someone is going to say before he or she says it? How often? With certain people?

6. Do you know anyone who often ends your sentences for you? How do you feel about it? Do you do it too?

When Mary Gordon moved from a small city newspaper to managing editor of a daily newspaper in a much larger city, she had no idea how hard it was to "start at the top." Not only was she the first woman to be encountered in newspaper management by most of her co-workers, but she was also the "new kid on the block." Everybody else seemed to know what was going on in the organization but her, and nobody would tell her anything—at first.

"I lost no time in trying to plug into the grapevine," she said. "I had to do an awful lot of listening. I got into the habit of just walking around the newsroom and talking to people. I found that by listening to the little things, I began to get some feelings about the big things."

Everybody agrees one ought to listen, but few people are able to tell you how. In fact, everybody assumes you automatically ought to know how. Weren't you, as a child, always exhorted to "listen"? As a new employee, you "listen" some more. Finally, you achieve a position of responsibility where people have to listen to you. At last! Now you can start giving instructions and orders to others. You've waited a long time to get into this game; now you want to be the quarterback and call the plays.

But it doesn't take long to realize that the quarterback can't win the game alone. Unless he has a good receiver to catch his passes, his throwing is going to be wasted. In fact, since it is the receiver of the message who has to carry out instructions, the manager quickly becomes aware that receiving is as important, if not more important, than sending messages.

How good is your listening? Have you ever emerged from a session in your boss's office, grappling with the meaning of what was said? Was your lack of understanding caused by his being a poor sender or by your being a poor receiver? According to several studies, people spend 45 percent of their time listening, 30 percent talking, 16 percent reading, and 9 percent writing. We spend almost half our waking hours listening, but we may be completely unaware of the skills involved.

Good listeners are rare, in business and elsewhere. Why?

There are lots of reasons. Some of them have to do with the listening process itself.

Hearing is a physiological function. We are capable of hearing sounds in the immediate environment, but this doesn't mean that we are necessarily listening to them. Listening requires mental energy to sort and interpret the sounds. The difference between hearing and listening depends upon the degree to which the interpretation becomes conscious.

We are surrounded by auditory stimuli—the clack of a typewriter, piped-in music, conversations around us, a computer humming—but we *choose* which, if any, we want to listen to at any given moment. And this may change from moment to moment as one thing or another becomes more interesting to us. Sometimes our inner voices are the most interesting, and we do not listen consciously to outside sounds at all because our mental energies have been directed elsewhere.

SELECTIVE LISTENING

Good listening skills must be developed and the right decisions must be made about what you will actively listen to and interpret and what you will merely hear. In an average workday, there are innumerable choices, many of which occur subliminally. You may be sitting at a meeting and suddenly realize that you have no idea what has been said for the past five or ten minutes. At some point, the process of selective perception allowed you to "tune out" the voices and divert your mental energy. Understanding how this works will help you to understand why "nobody *listens* around here."

Selective perception is necessary to prevent information overload. The brain is able to process just so much information at any given time. Most people speak at 200 to 250 words per minute, so if you try to listen to three conversations at once, the wpm triples, and good listening becomes difficult.

Information overload is one of the hazards of modern life.

We are constantly bombarded from many sources. Selective perception enables us to ignore the sounds we cannot cope with and to concentrate on what is important. For example, someone with a one-track mind has the ability to concentrate on one thing at a time; he chooses and selects from a narrow range of stimuli to the point where he becomes oblivious to the environment. Selective listening also protects us from information that we don't want to have, for various reasons. Often, a particular bit of information may be painful to the ego, so we tune it out. However, this ostrichlike behavior can backfire and become destructive in the long run.

In order to protect their egos, some people refuse to listen to criticism. During a session at which a superior is trying to point out their weaknesses, an employee may be busy filtering out the negative part of the message, converting a warning that his work is unsatisfactory into "just a few hints to help me improve." Someone about to be put on probation has been known to ask his supervisor when he could expect a promotion. In this case, a supervisor often has no choice but to be blunt, for nothing less will dent this person's protective armor.

At the other extreme is the fragile ego that listens for slights and criticisms: "I know you're out to get me, but maybe if I can anticipate your attack, I can ward it off." He or she not only listens intently for the slightest negative comment but escalates anything mildly critical into an attack. Thus, "you made an error on this account" is converted into, "You don't think I should have this job, do you?" The person in the weak position seizes the advantage, thus putting the supervisor on the defensive. The only defense is to refuse to play the game according to this employee's rules, and constantly tell him or her that they're giving you inaccurate feedback.

Are these examples recognizable, even though they are extreme? Since everyone has these tendencies, it's important to understand them in order to recognize whether you are distorting the messages that you listen to. The overly self-confident may not hear the criticism, whereas the overly self-effacing may hear criticism when none is intended. The key is to interpret correctly by listening accurately.

Selective listening works positively and negatively. When selective perception becomes too efficient, it can lead farther and farther away from reality and trigger a *defense reaction*.

Perhaps you, as a supervisor, have warned an employee that his volume of work is low. Instead of accepting this criticism and trying to improve, he blames you for giving him too much to do. From here, it's only a short step for him to assign a motive to your action: You don't like him and you're out to get him fired. From then on, anything you say is interpreted as persecution. He thinks, "What's the use trying if the boss is against me; I can't win." His work performance slumps further. He may be fired, thereby "proving" that he was right all along—you were out to get him fired and you succeeded.

Defense reactions protect the ego from pain but change nothing in the real world outside. Sooner or later, the world has a way of forcing the individual to confront it. It is the rare individual who can become aware of his or her own defense reactions without counseling, although awareness that such reactions exist may keep us on our guard against them. In counseling subordinates, the manager should try to help them become aware of their own defense reactions, if he hears any, before they get out of hand. (Counseling subordinates is covered in detail in Chapter 10.)

MIND SET AND PERCEPTION

Habits of perception are culturally derived and are learned at a very early age. Therefore, culturally derived perceptions unconsciously color everything we take in through our senses. One name for this is "mind set." The mind set has an enormous influence on what we perceive. The typical mind set of a white, Protestant, middle-class male will be different from the mind set of a Black,

Catholic, working class female. Everything that is heard is filtered through the mind set of the particular culture in which you happened to be raised. Recognizing that not everyone shares our particular mind set is often the first step in overcoming difficulties in communication.

Prejudice against racial, religious, or national groups or against one sex or the other is the product of extreme mind sets that indeed transcend reality. The job of rater in insurance companies has traditionally been held by women, but now with more flexibility in the job market, the traditional job roles are breaking down. When an insurance company in a large southern city hired its first male rater, the rumor had spread before he had even reported for work that he was a homosexual. The spurious "reasoning" must have gone like this: rating is a "feminine" job; homosexuals are effeminate males; therefore, a male rater is a homosexual.

Everybody has prejudices because everybody has some form of mind set. But rational people modify their culturally given mind sets in response to the real world. Our mind sets are carryovers from our childhood and our parents' influence. But the world changes, and these teachings may no longer be true, if indeed they ever were. Unless you want to live in an illusory world, you need to check your old mind sets against what's happening now. Unfortunately, an extremely prejudiced person is too busy protecting what he or she "knows" to learn anything new. Prejudice continually reinforces itself.

CORRECTIVE LISTENING

Selective perception and prejudice can lead to poor listening habits. But habits are learned, and they can be unlearned. The following poor listening habits can be easily corrected, once identified. See if you can see yourself doing them on a day-to-day basis. Ask yourself, "How often do I do that?"

1. *Frozen evaluation of the sender.* Unfortunately, once we make up our mind about another person, it usually

stays made up. We tend to type people, such as "office clown," "sexpot," "stubborn bulldog," and the typing sticks. If you have evaluated someone negatively in the past or have maintained a low opinion of someone for a long time, you may be guilty of "frozen evaluation" of that individual. You will probably tend to discount the person's messages as stupid or irrelevant and overlook any good ideas because your frozen evaluation has blocked your judgment.

The obverse is the positive frozen evaluation. You may have people reporting to you about whom you feel so positively that when these people bring you a message, you turn off your "active listening" and place greater value on the message than it deserves. You are too instantly accepting to be listening closely.

2. *Second-guessing the sender.* Are you one of those people who interrupt and finish sentences for others? In an effort to let the speaker know that they understand, these people take away his privilege of expressing himself. Often, when we think that we know someone well, especially if it is someone we want to please, we second-guess what that person is about to say and consequently miss the message entirely. The speaker may be too polite or too embarrassed to correct us, and the receiver has only his bad listening habits to blame.

3. *Premature closing.* Closely related to second-guessing is the habit of tuning out too soon, before the message is actually completed. The speaker says, "Please get me the Conners file and the figures on . . ." but before the speaker can finish, the receiver is on his way to get the file because he had stopped listening. Occasionally, the receiver will stop listening before an important qualifier at the end of a sentence. For example, "I'm not going out to lunch today unless I get this job done by noon," will be heard as "I'm not going out to lunch today" by a receiver who stopped listening too soon. Later, the receiver may be indignant to see the sender lunching with someone else at his favorite restaurant.

4. *Not listening as a status symbol.* Unfortunately, people of higher status in an organization often let employees know who's in command by interrupting them, not answering their questions, not following up on their topics, or substituting topics of their own. In our society, we view the person in charge as the one who does most of the talking. One way you can demonstrate you're "in charge" is to talk instead of listen.

Studies show that in male-female groups men do most of the talking. They also interrupt women more often than women interrupt men. Conversational topics introduced by men are developed further three times as often as topics introduced by women. Obviously, these are power tactics; the person who interrupts asserts his power by violating the other person's right to speak. In business, status may be a more important factor in this kind of behavior than sex. Traditionally, men have enjoyed higher status than women, and it is reasonable that status rather than sex determines who has the floor. When a woman has higher status, she would presumably tend to talk more and interrupt more. To understand the messages others send, the higher status person will have to discipline himself to listen, *not* to reinforce his status by not listening.

5. *Becoming distracted by the sender's delivery.* Although reading the nonverbal dimensions of a message is important, sometimes paying attention only to the way something is said can cause you to miss the verbal content. We once knew of an executive who paid a visit from corporate headquarters to motivate the employees at one of its small, rural plants. He was a dynamo—fast talking, with flailing gestures, flashy smile, and an overpowering handshake. Even though he said several important things, all the workers could remember was the way he presented himself. He accomplished nothing because nobody had heard a word he'd said. They were too overwhelmed by his mannerisms. To hear the message, you have to learn to tune out such distracting nonverbal cues.

6. *Prejudging the content of the message.* People can inhibit active listening by deciding in advance that they

don't like, are uninterested in, or don't agree with whatever subject is going to be discussed. However, if they had kept an open mind, they might have found that their prior assumptions were unfounded.

We have a friend who was preparing to go for a job interview and was convinced by a friend's warning that the personnel director would try to intimidate her. Thus she read challenges into everything the interviewer said and became so defensive that the interview was a total bomb. This would never have happened if she hadn't prejudged the content of the interviewer's message.

7. Overreacting to key words or phrases. Certain words or phrases carry loaded emotional meanings. Often, the receiver may react emotionally to the loaded words and miss the message. If a sender says "you're wrong," "that's a dumb idea," or "I certainly disagree with that," your defensive reaction can block your ability to listen actively. In addition to words with negative connotations, other words, although inoffensive to some, are "snarl words" to certain groups. Calling a middle-aged woman "girl" is an obvious example.

We know a manager who delights in playing devil's advocate, turning every conversation into an argument. Subordinates are on the defensive, and no one leaves with a good understanding of the other's position. When you find yourself reacting emotionally to the sender's words or tone, either ignore them or deal with them, but get them out of the way so that you can actively listen. You can parry the emotionally loaded comment with another question, such as "Why do you disagree?" or "Why did you call me a girl?" (The speaker may not be aware that he has offended, and this gives you an opportunity to point it out.)

8. Locking into your own viewpoint in an argument. When you get into an argument about something you feel strongly about, you tend to block out the opposing viewpoint. In fact, you tend to spend the time that your opponent is speaking in trying to formulate your next piece of supporting evidence. Yet this is the most important time to practice active listening. First, difficult as this is to believe, you may be wrong. In that case, the best way for you to win this argument would be to lose it. Second, by listening accurately, you may find a flaw in your opponent's argument that will enable you to win, or you may discover that you are both in agreement after all.

9. *Listening for too much detail.* Although it would seem to be a good thing to listen for as much information as possible, there are times when people "miss the forest for the trees." It is important not only to discern the separate pieces of the message, but also to pick up the major point being made. If you can't describe the major point in one sentence, you may have missed it.

10. *Wasting the difference in time between thought and speech.* Even though people are capable of processing from 200 to 250 words per minute, not everyone talks at that speed. Many people speak much slower. Most people have additional mental time on their hands while the sender is talking, and they can easily "tune out," finding other things, people, or thoughts more interesting.

Learning to become a better listener by correcting poor listening habits is the first step toward active listening, which is discussed in the next chapter.

EXERCISES

1. The next time you find yourself in an argument, do some self-analysis. Are you really listening to the other person's statements? What are you thinking about instead? Find an opportunity to initiate a second discussion. Maintain your emotional control and practice active listening. Evaluate the result.
2. Make a list of words or phrases that you like and dislike and identify the reasons why. Who do you know who commonly uses them? How do you feel about these

people's performance and capabilities. Are your feelings justified?

3. Make a list of mannerisms that annoy you. The next time you see someone use one, analyze what disturbs you about it. After the conversation, see how much you remember about what that person said. Were you distracted by the mannerism? Did you stop listening to the words?

4. The next time you have the floor in a conversation or meeting, time yourself. After a few minutes, stop and either ask a question or encourage your listener to question or comment. Do this for at least a week. Do you find that others understand you better?

5. The next time you find someone isn't paying full attention to your message, observe that person closely and try to identify the nonverbal messages you are getting that tell you he or she isn't really interested. Look for facial expression, indirect eye contact, quick movements, glancing down at a watch. And the next time you sense that *you're* not interested in what someone else is saying, stop and analyze what you are doing. Are you letting them know? How?

6. At your next meeting, don't take any notes. When the meeting is over, write down what you think the major points were. Then ask a co-worker to tell you what he or she thought. Compare similarities and discrepancies. Do the same for another meeting, but wait until a day or two later to write down your impressions of the main points. Compare them again with a co-worker. Did the time lapse make any difference? If the two of you selectively perceived differently, try to figure out why.

7. Someone in your circle of associates probably has the annoying habit of premature closing—interrupting the sender, finishing your sentences for you, etc. See if you can break this person of this habit by insisting upon completing your thought every time he or she interrupts. If the person is *yourself*, discipline yourself to allow the sender to finish his message.

5

Active Listening: The Key to Knowing What People Mean

"I certainly do wonder, Miss Melanctha," at last began Jeff Campbell, "I certainly do wonder, if we know very right, you and me, what each other is really thinking. I certainly do wonder, Miss Melanctha, if we know at all really what each other means by what we are always saying."
GERTRUDE STEIN, *Three Lives*
(New York: Random House, 1936)

PREVIEW

1. Do you tend to accept what people say at face value, or do you question what they really mean?

2. Who are the people at work you like and get along with unusually well? Do you listen to them differently than you listen to others? How?

3. Do you think of yourself as an empathetic person? Why or why not? Is this important on the job?

4. Have you ever acted on someone's secondhand report, only to find out later that it was inaccurate? Did you learn anything about listening from this experience?

5. Do you know how to ask the kind of questions that will elicit the information you want?

When we listen passively, the brain is only minimally engaged. In active listening, it is fully engaged. The difference is accounted for by the amount of mental energy that is invested. Passive listening is characterized by low mental energy, and it's caused either by low interest or by low physical energy. As we all know, on days when we're tired or coming down with a cold, we are not able to concentrate on anything very well. Anxiety or nervousness also interferes with our ability to concentrate on the messages we receive.

At work, people often listen passively, and they do so for several reasons. They may think nothing of importance is being said, so there's really no payoff for intense listening. Or they may have other sources of information that are more accurate. Or they depend on someone else to clarify messages and tell them what they really mean. Whatever the reason, the passive listener is a poor partner in communication.

Active listening, on the other hand, greatly increases the chances of seeing and hearing the real message, and it increases the feedback to the sender. Feedback is essential to the sender's success in getting his message across, and helping him to clarify his message is one of the things a good listener does.

In order to become an active listener, you must learn to:

1. Successfully block out competing messages.
2. Concentrate intensely on the message sender.
3. Be and act attentive.
4. Listen in context.
5. Give verbal and nonverbal feedback.
6. Use perceptual checks (testing your perception against the speaker's intention).
7. Distinguish between the cognitive (informational) and the affective (emotional) portions of the message and know how to listen to both.
8. Exercise your inference-making ability.

The first four points above are easiest to accomplish. Blocking out competing messages and concentrating are relatively easy if you can guarantee a quiet environment, whether a private office or conference room, a carpeted boardroom, a cozy restaurant, or even the relative isolation of a golf course. Whenever possible, choose an environment for communication that will encourage active listening, both your own and others'.

Attentive behavior always encourages active listening. This subject is dealt with at greater length in chapter 9, but, briefly, it entails signaling the speaker that you are paying close attention by sitting alertly, leaning forward slightly, and, from time to time, making eye contact with him. These "I'm listening" signals encourage the speaker, who's more likely to send better messages if he or she doesn't have to use extra energy to gain your attention. Remember, too, that words are defined by their context. If you are listening attentively, you will catch those subtle differences in meaning inherent in the context of the speaker's words.

The remaining keys to active listening are the focus of the rest of this chapter. Learn and use them—they are the keys to successful communication.

FEEDBACK AND PERCEPTUAL CHECKS

Speakers rely on their audience to let them know when their messages aren't getting through. Feedback can be in the form of head-nodding, noncommittal "un-huhs," or "Go on, I'd like to hear more." If the listener neglects giving the cues, the speaker will interpret this as a negative reaction. In the jargon of behaviorists, nonreinforcement leads to extinction; in other words, the speaker who is not receiving feedback tends to clam up.

Through the *perceptual check*, a special type of feedback, you can test your perception of the message against the speaker's intention. If you have been actively listening, but the information begins to seem fuzzy, conflicting, or abstract, stop the speaker and rephrase what he or she has just said. For example: "Let me be sure I understand you. Are you saying that we're risking a lawsuit if we do this?" If the sender agrees that this was the intent of the message, the point is clarified. If the sender disagrees, then it becomes his or her responsibility to clarify. Of course, if the sender is purposely trying to be vague or abstruse, no amount of perceptual checking will clarify the message, and you may have to remain in the dark.

NONVERBAL CLUES TO EMOTIONS

Before reacting to a speaker, however, you must first decide what you will react to. All messages have both cognitive (informational) and affective (emotional) content. Which is the most important part of the message? Whichever it is, this is what you must listen to most attentively, and you will probably need to indicate to the sender which you are paying attention to.

It is often difficult to read the emotional content of messages, especially when they come from executives and managers. Usually the higher the status of the person, the more skilled he or she has become in hiding his or her true feelings behind a smokescreen of seemingly rational messages.

What can you do to discern the true feelings of the sender? Often, nonverbal behavior is the best clue. For instance, a co-worker delivers an innocuous-sounding message, but his eyes flash with anger. Obviously the emotional message is more important than the informational one, although the sender may deny it. (Have you ever heard someone declare, "I'm not angry," but his voice quivers with rage?) Appropriate feedback might be: "You seem upset. Is something the matter?"

From then on, the ball is in the other person's court. He or she may deny any emotion, reveal that the topic under discussion is upsetting, or that the cause is some personal matter which he or she may or may not want to discuss. Then the sender and receiver must decide whether to continue the original conversation, discuss whatever it is that is bothering this person instead, or postpone the discussion until some later time.

What happens if you ignore the emotional message? Perhaps nothing, but consider a hypothetical situation. Suppose an employee hears through the grapevine of a possible realignment in his department and fears a demotion. He is naturally defensive, but you reassure him that he's mistaken. You have not only relieved his anxiety, but you've averted a problem that could have built up pressure toward some future explosion.

When nonverbal and verbal messages conflict, the non-verbal one usually carries the emotion and is the true one. Some managers who want to look "only at the facts" tend to forget that the way a worker feels about something on the job is also a fact.

MESSAGES: FACTS VS. FALLACIES

Many messages that appear to be fact are anything but. Since language can conceal as well as reveal meanings, it pays to cultivate a healthy skepticism while listening. Unfortunately, many messages contain common deceptions, like those listed below, that may or may not be intentional. (For advice on how to use some of these devices positively to aid communication, see Chapter 9.)

1. *Vagueness and generalities.* "Everybody says," "They say," "Most companies have found . . ." Vague language is often couched in the passive voice ("It is believed," "The deed was accomplished.") The sentence has no subject and no initiator of the action is named. This can be a very convenient dodge for evading responsibility.

Some speakers manage to combine vagueness with the logical fallacy called "begging the question," inviting the listener to accept as true what remains to be proved. Example: "It is well understood by people in the field that . . ." What is "well understood," and by whose definition? Who are these people? (This sort of thing may be permissible when a person with expert knowledge is asked for an opinion and can back up the opinion with facts.)

2. *Verbal overkill.* When anything even slightly above average is called "fantastic," what is the truly extraordinary? Advertising has conditioned all listeners to expect overstatement: "the movie of the century," "the greatest car ever made." Just don't, as a listener, over-react to this verbal habit or you'll think the sky is falling when it isn't. Is this really a "crisis" or just an everyday problem? Is this

mistake really "catastrophic," this person really a "disaster," this idea really "earth-shaking?" On the other hand, you must not be so skeptical that you ignore warnings of a real disaster. Careful listening and questioning are essential to making a correct judgment.

3. *Euphemisms.* Euphemisms are socially useful words and phrases that cloak naked realities in dress that makes them fit for polite company. For instance, no one "rests" in restrooms. By calling it a "protective reaction," politicians were able to get the American public to overlook the fact that people in southeast Asia were being bombed. And a politician was applauded for doing nothing by calling it "creative restraint."

If both sender and receiver agree on the meaning of the euphemism, no harm is done. Sometimes there is tacit agreement to call one thing by another name for reasons of mutual face-saving. No doubt it does feel better to be "selected out" rather than "fired." But sometimes, euphemisms are deceptive. Be especially skeptical about any pleasant-sounding phrase whose meaning is vague. It's OK to call shoplifting "inventory shrinkage" so long as we realize that we're being robbed blind and we need to do something—but not if the euphemism gives us the feeling that it's something inevitable and beyond our control.

4. *Name calling.* Name calling is a way that many people can avoid thinking and persuade others to join them in the same habit. If the radical left calls somebody a "fascist," the radical right can call other people "communists." But what real meaning do these have? Or these: "flaming liberal," "women's libber," "male chauvinist," "egghead," "bleeding heart?" Usually, very little.

5. *Clichés, metaphors, and stock phrases.* At first glance, clichés and metaphors would seem to be worlds apart. But most clichés began as metaphorical expressions. They were once fresh, colorful, and clever, but repetition wore them out. Clichés are great timesavers because they

require no imagination, and often the lazy sender will use one whether or not it's appropriate to the message. The cliché, if not misleading, is often vague or meaningless. Does "game plan" mean some special kind of strategy? Does "let's go through channels" mean "let's not upset anybody by going around him," or does it conceal something such as a dislike for trying a new method?

6. *Irrelevancies.*   Are the facts that you're listening to relevant to the topic? Do the statistics being cited in an oral presentation really make any difference in the total budget? Asking yourself relevancy questions as you listen will save you from endless streams of drivel that have nothing to do with the subject. Also, by discouraging irrelevancies, you signal the sender that you're interested in *quality,* not quantity of information.

7. *Logical fallacies.*   *Fallacies* in logic must be guarded against. Among the most common are *hasty generalizations,* in which the speaker jumps to a general conclusion based on inconclusive evidence; *post hoc,* in which the cause of something is attributed to a factor that's purely coincidental; *false analogy,* in which two dissimilar situations are compared and conclusions drawn as if they were identical; and evasive action by an *appeal to the emotions.* Here's an example of emotional appeal in action:

SUPERVISOR: I can't recommend you for promotion just yet. You need to show more initiative.
EMPLOYEE: I'll never be promoted. Everybody knows women don't get anywhere in this company.

Unless the supervisor is careful, he or she may be diverted from the topic (the employee's initiative, or lack of it) to a generalized discussion of discrimination. The employee is appealing to the supervisor's guilt in order to evade a discussion of her own shortcomings.

INFERENCE-MAKING

A message is predominantly informational if its content can be ascertained objectively. A statement such as "the thermometer registers 32°F." can be verified by checking the thermometer. A message is predominantly affective if its content cannot be validated by another person. "He got the promotion through politics" is an example. Perhaps such statements can be supported by facts, but often, as in this example, such statements are opinions with built-in judgments. Presumably, a "political" promotion is bad, because of the negative connotation of the word *politics*.

Such predominantly subjective messages would present few problems in communications if they didn't frequently come to us disguised as informational, objective messages. The wary manager will not be misled into accepting a subordinate's subjective reports at face value.

In order to listen actively and to make sound judgments about what you hear, you need to become aware of the inferences people include in their reports to you. Often, people think that they are reporting what they see and hear, but actually they are reporting their *inferences* (or assumptions), which may or may not be accurate. Also, they may or may not be the same inferences that others make.

For example, "That son-of-a-bitch Johnson fouled up my order again" may or may not be factual, but it *is* a report of the speaker's feelings about Johnson. You could respond to this statement on the cognitive level by saying, "You seem to feel strongly about Johnson. How come?" It turns out that all he knows for sure is that he didn't get the right supplies and that Johnson usually fills his order. Ordinarily the inference that Johnson had sent the wrong supplies would be correct. But perhaps Johnson was out sick that day and someone else filled the order. In that case, the inference was incorrect because a vital fact was missing.

There is certainly nothing wrong with inference-making, but you must be conscious of what you are listening to— facts or inferences—in order to draw correct conclusions.

An inference is a probability, not a certainty, and usually many different inferences can be made about the same fact or observation.

Fact: Mr. X., a vice-president who usually speaks to you on the elevator, doesn't speak this morning.
Inference 1:   Mr. X. is angry at you.
Inference 2:   Mr. X. is really a snob, and now he's showing his true colors.
Inference 3:   Mr. X. is preoccupied about a decision he has to make and didn't even see you.
Inference 4:   Mr. X. doesn't feel well this morning.
Then Mr. X.'s secretary happens to mention to you that Mr. X. went to the eye doctor this morning before work. So,
Inference 5:   Mr. X. had drops in his eyes and couldn't see you.

In another case, perhaps you notice (infer) that a co-worker seems to be upset about something. You interpret his expression as "worried." But perhaps he simply had a sleepless night or is recovering from an illness or a hangover. Unless you investigate further, you don't know for sure. You can create many problems when you act on your inferences as if they were certainties. By asking questions, you can draw out the facts behind the inferences and avoid an action that you may later regret.

It should be plain by now that if you're actively listening, you'll be constantly asking yourself questions: "What does he have to back up that statement?" "Is this point relevant to what he's trying to prove?" "What does that word mean the way he's using it now?" Additionally, the active listener will also be asking questions out loud in an attempt to clarify the speaker's meaning. Not that the active listener is always interrupting, but whenever he finds the message becoming vague or confusing, he will ask questions that let the sender know that he's off-target. The active listener helps the speaker by asking what he needs to know in order to understand the message.

Some of the types of questions we've already covered include the *affective check*, which asks about emotions; the *inference check*, which asks for the facts behind the inference; and the *perceptual check*, which is designed to check the listener's perception of the message against the speaker's intentions.

MOTIVATING THROUGH ACTIVE LISTENING

One of your purposes as a manager is to understand your people well enough to be able to motivate them. Since what motivates one person will not move another, learning what each person will respond to requires listening, *active listening;* it requires getting on the same wavelength with that person. Another word that describes being on the same wavelength is *empathy.*

We usually have empathy with only a few people, perhaps with a spouse or close friends. When you are empathetic with someone, you actually enter into his or her mental processes. You can literally guess what the other person will say before he says it. People who relate on this level need fewer words and symbols. Sometimes, in moments when you are concentrating hard on a fellow-worker, your active listening skills can become so acute that you become temporarily empathetic.

Traditionally, human relations in business have been impersonal and formalized. In many ways, they will continue to be, because everyone has a role to play. But younger workers increasingly expect more personal satisfaction from their work. The work environment and the relationships among workers is a major source of job satisfaction. People will be motivated to produce more in a setting in which they feel they are understood and valued. Even if the boss's understanding is less than perfect, the mere fact that he listens actively and shows that he is trying to understand is perceived by subordinates as demonstrating their worth. The manager who is a good listener and takes co-workers seriously provides a real morale booster.

In contrast, the nonlistening manager who brushes people off is saying nonverbally, "You don't really matter to me." People treated like this usually respond by becoming less productive. If their contributions aren't that important, why bother? Likewise, the manager who becomes angry when he receives bad news is teaching his co-workers to tell him only what he wants to hear. His chances of getting accurate feedback and information will be nil.

To get the most from their people, managers must practice active listening and demonstrate receptivity. It is also good policy to encourage others to become active listeners as well. Many times misunderstandings arise that could have been prevented if *both* parties had been listening actively. Management must encourage employees to ask questions, to check their perceptions, and to give feedback—in a word, to practice active listening. Among the ways to do this are:

1. Set a good example by being an active listener yourself.

2. Ask subordinates for their feedback on your messages. Create an atmosphere of acceptance and receptivity, both verbally and nonverbally. There's no use asking, "Are there any questions?" when your tone of voice makes it plain that questions are not welcome. "Are there any questions?" is too vague anyway. The answer will almost always be no. Be more specific and ask questions like "What's the most important thing we need to do?"

3. Watch subordinates for nonverbal cues on whether they're listening. If you suspect they're not actively listening, stop talking and ask questions.

4. Resist the temptation to do all the talking and pause periodically to encourage subordinates to give you their perceptual checks. Get them in the habit of re-stating your messages in their own words. If you let them know you expect a perceptual check, they will listen more carefully.

5. Teach your subordinates about multiple inferences. Get them in the habit of checking their inferences against

facts in order to improve the quality of their information gathering.

6. Share (exchange) inferences with them. Train them in evaluating inferences. How dependable are they? If several inferences are possible, which is most probable and why?

7. Take a listening course or encourage your subordinates to take one. Many are available on tape.

The mere fact that you care enough to listen actively to others and that you care whether or not your staff knows how to listen carefully and correctly ought to raise the level of awareness of what is most often the weakest link in the chain of communication.

EXERCISES

1. Initiate a lengthy conversation with someone who usually bores you. Practice active listening and see if your attitude changes toward this individual. See if you can identify the reasons why you perceived him or her as boring.

2. Practice the technique of perceptual check. In your next lengthy conversation with someone, interrupt him or her and check what you don't understand. Rephrase the message and ask them for clarification or confirmation. Do that every time you get confused and see if you come away with a better understanding.

3. Make a list of the employees who report to you and note what you think motivates that person: money, praise, recognition, being accepted as part of the group? If you don't know, actively listen to that person until you find out.

4. The next time you are chairing a meeting or giving instructions to others, periodically stop and ask for feedback to be sure everyone understands what you are saying. Ask "Are there any questions at this point?" "Would someone be willing to summarize that last point?" If you see that they are misunderstanding, find a different way to express the same idea or ask someone else to put it in their words.

6

Sending Nonverbal
Status Messages

You can observe a lot just by watching.
YOGI BERRA

PREVIEW

1. Do certain people in your office get too close to you
for comfort or touch you more than you like? Why does it
bother you? Why do they do it? Are they higher or lower in
status?

2. Do you ever sense that some people are uncomfortable in your presence, especially subordinates? Do you
know why?

3. Do you feel tense or awkward in the presence of
higher-status people in your company? Do you think they
know it? Is there something you can do to convey a more
relaxed manner?

4. Have you ever heard comments that reflect on your
ability or potential that contradict the way you know you
are inside? Why do people have this impression of you? Is
there anything you can do to change it?

5. Are there some people who seem to have trouble
"looking you in the eye?" What does this mean?

6. Are there any people in your company whose dress

seems especially "right" and others whose dress seems "wrong?" Why? Do you feel confident about your own way of dressing for the job?

A company president we know enjoys calling in groups of first-line supervisors for what he calls "informal chats." However, few of the supervisors consider them informal, and they are usually stiff and subdued in his presence. One day, the president took out a pack of cigarettes and proceeded to chain smoke during the discussion.

A very odd thing happened. The supervisors loosened up, relaxed, and began to talk with him more openly. He sometimes repeated the smoking on later occasions with similar results, but he never connected the two and couldn't figure out why some groups were more open with him than others. The supervisors, however, perceived the smoking as a flaw, a human weakness that made him seem more like one of them. ("He's human after all!") It operated unconsciously as a nonverbal cue that enabled them to relax and speak more freely.

NONVERBAL SIGNALS

The importance of nonverbal behavior should not be underestimated. Actions *do* speak louder than words. The nonverbal messages we send and receive may not be articulated as "He's nervous because I have higher status than he does," but rather experienced as vague feelings of discomfort in another person's presence and perhaps even dislike. These feelings are translated into inferences about coworkers, and unless you make the correct inferences and develop a sensitivity to nonverbal cues, your communication efforts will falter. You must learn to tune in on your subliminal impressions, then observe the other person's behavior and check your conclusions; in other words, you must become conscious of what is now mainly unconscious. This chapter will show specifically how status is conveyed nonverbally in business situations, and how your demeanor affects people's estimation of you and their responses to you.

Some of the most puzzling misunderstandings are caused by a failure to read body language. Realtors are all too familiar with the buyer who describes in precise detail exactly what he or she wants—and then won't buy it. Successful salespeople know that frequently a prospective -buyer will describe not what he wants but what he thinks he should want. The salesperson watches carefully for non-verbal reactions. If he sees negative reactions, the salesperson leads him, by skillful questioning, to reveal what he's really after. Or, he makes an educated guess and watches the reaction to his suggestions.

The successful salesperson always owes part of his or her success to the ability to read body language. Some call this "intuition." However, behavioral scientists have shown that much so-called intuition is really an unconscious awareness of subtle, nonverbal cues. The use of videotape and audio equipment has made it possible to capture and analyze these subliminal cues to human behavior. And often they are so minute that they can be seen only by studying motion picture film frame by frame.

STATUS BEHAVIOR IN BUSINESS

Probably no type of nonverbal behavior has received more attention than status. And nowhere is status easier to observe than in the business world. In a famous study, two social scientists made a series of ten silent films. Each film featured the same two characters, a man seated at a desk in a private office, telephoning, and a second man who entered the office and spoke to him. The variables in the films were how long it took the first man to put down the phone and greet his visitor; how long the second man hesitated before entering; and his manner of advancing toward the desk (how fast he moved, where he stopped).

People viewing the film were asked to rate the relative

status of the two men. There was wide agreement that the man behind the desk was of higher status if he took a longer time to acknowledge the other's presence, stayed on the phone longer, and remained seated while his visitor stood. The relative lowliness of status of the visitor was judged by where he stopped in his approach. He had the lowest status if he hesitated just inside the door and the highest if he walked straight up to the desk. The visitor was judged to have higher status than the first man if, when he walked up to the desk, the man on the phone put it down and rose immediately to greet him.

You've probably witnessed similar scenes every day and simply may not have given them any thought. But if you are to become a better communicator, recognizing and using nonverbal cues to status is a subject you can't afford *not* to think about, especially if you want to improve your own status in your company. Fitting a role is partly dependent on nonverbal communication of status.

In another experiment, subjects were asked by psychologists to pick out lower-status people. The psychologists found that the subjects based their judgments on such nonverbal cues as frequent nodding and smiling, holding the arms close to the body, and standing with legs closer together when talking to a higher-status person. More women than men exhibited this type of behavior; however, when the same women deliberately exhibited more "high-status" behavior, such as smiling only occasionally, holding their heads comparatively still, and standing in a more relaxed posture, both men and women judged that they held high-status jobs—whether or not they actually did. Exhibiting such "low-status" behavior may encourage people to think of you as suited for low-status jobs, while acting more like a high-status person may encourage others to think of you as suited for higher-status jobs.

This is just one example of the practical applications of a knowledge of nonverbal cues. The ability to read and send the right cues will also prevent you from unwittingly offending the higher-status players of the corporate game.

NONVERBAL CUES TO STATUS

Status cues in business are conveyed by the same means of nonverbal communication that convey all other cues. These include facial expressions, gestures, posture, body movements, dress, hairstyle, and voice cues, such as tones of voice, loudness, and pitch. While most of these are visual cues (hence the expression "reading" another person), some important vocal cues depend on the listener's picking up subtle variations in sounds that are not strictly needed to understand the content of the message.

Status can also be communicated by space. Usually, higher-status persons have more space at their disposal; their offices are larger, have more windows and the most desirable locations in the building. They also occupy more personal space; their invisible "bubbles" are bigger and they invade others' space more frequently. Such use of space to indicate status in the hierarchy is typical of traditional organizations.

Another example: Envision a typical corporate board room, furnished with a long, rectangular table and chairs. One end is customarily the head of the table and may have a slightly different type of chair. The highest-ranking person present will be expected to sit at the head position.

Suppose, however, that a group of strangers enters the room. The person who sits at the head of the table will most likely be treated as if he or she were in charge—merely by occupying the space recognized by custom as pre-eminent. (This is exactly what happens in jury rooms. The person sitting at or near the head of the table is most likely to be elected foreman.)

No single nonverbal cue can be pulled out of context and interpreted in isolation. Rather, a cluster of behaviors, working together, conveys meaning that the receiver of the message "gets" (usually subliminally) in a split second. Don't believe the popular books that interpret the meaning of a single bit of body language, such as crossed arms signifying "disagreement" or a woman sitting with legs apart meaning "availability." Other behavioral cues must back up this interpretation, so be cautious.

Think back to the stereotyped businessman in Chapter 3. The stereotype is male, not female. His uniform, the business suit, needs no description. Certain facial characteristics (light skin, hair, and eyes) and body type (tall and lean) also come to mind. His face will be relatively expressionless, his posture erect (and perhaps a little rigid), his gestures limited to those close to his body and a little stiff. If his voice is also deep and thus "authoritative," the picture is complete. When people are asked to evaluate high-status and low-status behavior, they have this stereotype in mind as their high-status ideal. And it isn't accidental that most American business leaders look the part. Those who don't fit the stereotype will have to compensate in other ways—in nonverbal ways. For instance, short people can look taller by drawing themselves up to their full height and by using eyes, face, and voice authoritatively.

However, success in business doesn't necessarily require exhibiting stereotypic high-status behavior. In some business situations—in sales, for instance—exhibiting higher-status behavior is pure folly. The successful salesperson knows better than to outshine his customer, and in fact he may deliberately tone down his dress and behavior. And don't confuse high *status* with *leadership*. Some high-status persons are mere figureheads; the real leadership comes from elsewhere.

STATUS INTERACTIONS IN
BUSINESS

The following are some of the characteristic behaviors of higher-status persons in business. Bear in mind that all are *relative* to the other person or persons in the interaction.

1. *The higher-status person determines the distance between people who are interacting,* either by approaching

the other person himself or by indicating how close the other person should come. Relative distance was the chief means by which viewers determined status in the silent-movie experiments. This has to do with management of what social scientists call "personal space."

Each person is enclosed in an "invisible bubble" of personal space, which is the amount of "breathing room" needed to interact comfortably with others. Too much space is interpreted as formality, coldness, or dislike, while too little is felt to be threatening or intimate, depending on whether the other person is a rival co-worker or a lover. For our culture, two to four feet between people is a comfortable distance for business transactions. The lower-status person who approaches any closer than that to the higher-status person is apt to be put in his place for "pushiness."

On the other hand, the higher-status person is free to reinforce his status by invading the other's personal space—by thrusting his own face close to the other's or by poking or jabbing at him with forefinger, pipe, or pencil. But if the higher-status person wishes to honor the lower-status person by making him an intimate, he may beckon him closer with a crook of the forefinger so that they can "put their heads together." The more a higher-status person has literally "kept his distance," the more flattering it is when he or she finally comes closer.

The distances preferred by Americans are far from universal. Businessmen from Arab cultures, for example, do not feel comfortable during interaction unless they can literally feel each other's breath, while Latin Americans also interact closely. These behaviors apply to nationalities and to ethnic groups. If discomfort is experienced in interactions between people in your office, it may in part be caused by differing expectations about the correct distances for interaction.

2. *The higher-status person will be in a higher physical position.*   In many societies, nobody's head can be higher than the king's. Even in our democratic times, there is an unconscious feeling that the person of higher status should

be placed above the lower. Executives who want to send "status" messages sometimes arrange to have their desks placed on platforms, whereas tall salespersons, whose height places them too far "above" their purchasing agent-customers, might have to sit slouched down in a chair or be thought too intimidating. Speakers use height instinctively, standing to lecture (the more authoritative mode) and sitting to receive questions. Height automatically places one member of the interchange above the other. If there are three people in the interchange, the two taller persons can talk above the shorter one's head, effectively excluding him. (The shorter person needs to compensate—probably by inviting the others to sit down.)

When you approach employees at their desk, do you sometimes "stand over" them, watching them work? If you are a higher-status person, you may be intimidating them without meaning to. You "hover over" someone as a threat, but sit down next to them to talk at eye level if you want to put them at ease.

3. *The higher-status person will be less tense in posture, voice, and gestures.* People tend to become tense in the presence of those of higher status, particularly when they expect to be evaluated in some way. In a classic series of experiments in social psychology, the subject moved closer to the experimenter who has just given him a favorable report about himself (or whom he expects to) and farther away from the experimenter who gives or is about to give him a negative report. Since this tension is inevitable, it becomes the higher-status person's responsibility to put the lower-status person at ease.

4. *The higher-status person calls the conversational shots.* He or she begins and ends discussions, does more of the talking, interrupts more frequently, and gives fewer "attending behavior" signals. Frequent smiling and head nodding, interpreted as low-status behaviors, are of course forms of "attending behaviors," in which one person says to another nonverbally, "I'm listening." Since lower-status persons will not interrupt you or tell you that you talk too

much, it becomes the higher-status person's responsibility to control his or her behavior in conversation—or suffer the consequences of poor communication.

5. *Higher-status people touch lower-status people more than lower-status people touch them.* Touching in American society is closely linked with either sex or aggression, so much so that even in crowded public places where touching is unavoidable, people can be observed pulling themselves back tightly into their own bodies and avoiding eye contact. It's taboo even for close friends to do much touching, particularly if both are males.

Despite these taboos, a certain amount of touching does go on in a business setting, such as pats on the back or a restraining hand placed on someone's arm while talking. Unless the two are of equal status, the person initiating the action is undoubtedly of higher status. Does the file clerk slap the vice-president on the back? Of course not. No matter how gentle the touch, the backslap says nonverbally, "I'm of higher status than you because I can touch you, but you can't touch me unless I permit it." This status message does not, however, rule out the possibility that the toucher really does have warm feelings of affection or good will toward the person being touched.

Women in business may interpret touching as sexual (and it could be), but it might be a ploy for either establishing or maintaining dominance. Studies have shown that males in business touch females more frequently than females touch males. Touching by women is often confusing to men because it may be a bid for equal status. Similarly, if a woman bristles at a male co-worker's touch, he should stop. She's probably interpreting it as a subtle put-down.

6. *The higher-status person engages the lower-status person in eye contact more steadily and more frequently.* In fact, eye contact could be regarded as a form of touching. In any dominant/submissive pair, the dominant person looks boldly at the submissive person, who looks away. (Historically, this was the eye behavior taught to men and women in Western European cultures. Check it

out by looking at past century paintings of lovers: he looks into her eyes; she casts her eyes down demurely.) This kind of behavior is also widely exhibited on the job.

Our culture makes much of the ability to "look someone in the eye" as a sign of trustworthiness, whereas many cultures teach that this is rude. As a higher-status person, don't judge downcast eyes too harshly if the other person is from another culture. This person may be merely exhibiting politeness. And it also behooves you, the lower-status person, to overcome your early training and learn to look people in the eye.

7. *Facial expressions will tend to be more controlled in higher-status persons.* Whereas frequent smiling was judged to be low-status behavior (probably because a smile is one way of placating), some higher-status persons will wear frowning, "threatening" faces, which may signal status insecurity. Even more common is the expressionless mask cultivated by the successful person who knows that it is often advantageous to conceal one's feelings.

Facial expressions are among the most universal of signals, and the easiest to bring under conscious control, as will be demonstrated in Chapter 7.

8. *Higher and lower status are frequently inferred from voice stereotypes.* Many cultures distinguish between "high prestige" and "low prestige" speech. Archie Bunker's speech places him immediately as a Northeastern working-class white, while Laurence Olivier's polished tones are definitely upper-class British.

Unfortunately, a person entering business with an accent from a low-prestige group will be awarded lower status automatically. (Nobody would hire Archie Bunker to sell jewelry at Tiffany's because his voice says Woolworth's.) Just how low the assigned status will be depends upon the expectations of his listeners; investment bankers will expect higher-prestige speech than general contractors, for example. One finding of researchers is that listeners can and do identify socio-economic background from speech alone and that they tend to assign negative personality traits to people identified as being from low-prestige groups.

American society, like every other, has culturally shared assumptions about the personality traits that go with specific voice qualities. The casting director knows he needs a gruff-voiced actor for macho parts and a sultry-voiced actress for the seductive female lead. Unfortunately for women, Americans have long typecast deep, loud male voices as indicators of authority in business, whereas a loud female voice, if high pitched, usually becomes shrill and is less authoritative than a softer voice. Women must learn to cultivate a tone of firmness, and both women and men whose voices are high pitched often must learn to lower the pitch.

Listeners should be aware of how much they may be influenced by their unconscious assumptions about character based on voice cues. Often vocal stereotypes work as self-fulfilling prophecies. For many years, women were not hired as radio and TV newscasters because "women's voices lack authority." However, as soon as women broadcast journalists began giving the news, they became authorities, and their voices began being considered authoritative.

9. *The quickest status cue is clothing (together with hair styling, makeup, and grooming).* Dress not only signifies occupation (the chef's hat, the lab technician's white coat) and role (the switch from business suit to tennis shorts signals a shift from work to leisure roles), but the status associated with occupation and role (overalls as a work uniform versus a business suit). In large organizations, which tend to be anonymous and impersonal, people will tend to treat you the way they perceive you. And what they perceive first of all is a general impression of clothing-makeup-hair, which forms your image.

In John T. Molloy's bestselling *Dress for Success*, he proved that "people who look successful and well educated receive preferential treatment." First, he sent out men in "lower-middle-class business suits," and again dressed in "upper-middle-class" suits. In the "push test," his men dressed in "upper garments" were allowed to go ahead through a revolving door, while the same men dressed in "lower" garments were pushed aside. In another experiment, his men were able to give orders to somebody else's secretary when dressed in "upper" garb.

One of Molloy's most interesting findings was the wide agreement on the status levels of various types of clothing, even among people who do not wear this clothing themselves. Thus the pinstriped business suit is perceived as an upper-middle-class garment not only by the upper-middle-class businessmen who wear these suits, but by those who never do. The advice given to men in management is simple: Find someone who dresses well at the job level *above* yours and use him as a model. Women managers looking for role models have a problem, as Molloy pointed out in his second book, *Women's Dress for Success Book*. Like men, however, women should dress *up* to the higher-status role. No matter how a man dresses, he will not be mistaken for a secretary, but a woman will, unless her image sends unmistakable status messages. Women are advised to carry briefcases (a symbol that goes with business status) not only to business meetings but to cocktail lounges and restaurants when traveling. Under no circumstances, say the experts, can a woman building a career afford to look either sexy or cute: no low-cut dresses, slit skirts, or heavy makeup.

Two psychologists who run "image workshops" ask each member in the workshop to write a quick impression of the others. Each member then compares these impressions with his or her own statement of the image they want to project. While we recognize and use society's stereotypes in evaluating others—gray hair is old on women, distinguished on men—it is difficult to apply these same stereotypes to ourselves. After all, we know how we really are—inside. Thus a blonde woman in her twenties who sold advertising felt knowledgeable and professional, but others told her that she looked like a "kewpie doll." To look more professional, she had to shorten her hair style, tone down her rosy makeup, and wear tailored clothes. Since nonverbal status messages are often self-fulfilling prophecies, the most important person to observe may be yourself.

EXERCISES

1. Keep a chart for recording nonverbal behavior of everyone you come in contact with for a week. Write the name, age and sex of each, then try to think of a descriptive word or two under the following nonverbal categories: *eye contact, posture, walk, facial expression, voice, clothing* and *other.*

If possible, observe the same person in your presence and also in the presence of one or two others of different age, sex, and status from yourself. Notice any differences? Are you picking up any status cues? Do they go with this person's job? What information do you have about this person that you were not aware of before?

2. Notice whether any people in your organization seem to invade other's personal space—leaning over them, pointing with pen or cigar, poking, etc. What is their status? How are they regarded by others? Try it yourself, and see if the person moves away.

3. Observe daily dress in three to six people of different status for a week. Is there anyone who seems successful in spite of what he or she wears? Can you identify a preferred type of dress, a "corporate image?" Is there someone whose dress is unusually fashionable? What kind of job does he or she have? Share your judgments with others and compare their reactions with yours. Are there differences of opinion about dress based on the age, sex, or status of the perceivers?

7

Listening to Body Language

Man is read in his face.
BEN JONSON

PREVIEW

1. Is there someone in your organization who is especially good at sizing up strangers? Do you know how he or she does it?

2. Do you consider yourself to be an introvert or an extrovert? Why?

3. Can you often tell when someone is lying? How often are you right? If you're often right, how did you know?

4. Do you sometimes find awkward pauses in your conversations? Does a conversation sometimes languish and die without your knowing why?

5. Are you sometimes accused of being a poor listener even though you heard every word? What are you missing?

6. Do you often feel empathy for another person when you are communicating? Is there any nonverbal behavior that seems to go with this feeling?

7. Is there someone you know who is particularly adept at putting people at ease? Do you know how it is done?

The verbal content of a message is neither the total message nor is it always the most important part. Since words are often used to hide feelings, what is *not* said (but may be read in the speaker's body, face, voice, or use of space) may be a more reliable guide to how a person really feels. Some old popular songs have lyrics that, although corny, often express a true message: "Every little movement has a meaning all its own," or "Your lips tell me 'no, no,' but there's 'yes, yes' in your eyes." When verbal and nonverbal messages conflict, the nonverbal message is often the true one.

However, to say that "the body doesn't lie" is to oversimplify. If you happen to be a successful clinical psychologist, mother, trial lawyer, salesperson, or gambler, it may be more difficult to fool you, since these occupations train people to read body language as a key to success. But bodies can and do lie, and some people are good actors indeed.

Recently, we watched a young athlete, a runner, being interviewed on television. He was very articulate and beautifully controlled. But when the camera zoomed back for a longer shot, we saw that one of his legs was jiggling up and down in double time to his speech, giving away his nervousness. It is often just such incongruities that give a person away, and that the astute watcher can observe and utilize.

NONVERBAL LANGUAGE

Managers, too, engage in confrontations and negotiations in which it helps to know what all the factors at play are. Both one-to-one and one-to-group interactions will go more smoothly if you learn to pick up emotional indicators from body language.

Have you ever given a co-worker some bad news and had him or her accept it with a smile, only to learn later that he or she was furious? Or have you had a co-worker smilingly agree with all your instructions, but then not carry them out? (The smile was a mask to hide his confusion.) As a manager, you must be aware of masks: the eyes that remain fixed even though the lips smile, or the flickering expression of anger or puzzlement that flashes across the smiling face.

The culture also teaches hand, arm and body gestures. Some gestures have an agreed upon meaning (the thumb in the air of the hitchhiker in our culture, for example) while others merely accompany speech. Americans use only about thirty such gestures, whereas Latin cultures use many, so crosscultural misunderstandings can occur. You may think an employee "emotional" only because his culture is more gestural.

Each sex learns the kind of nonverbal behavior expected by the culture. Although women are allowed to touch each other more, in mixed groups they are expected to talk less than men, to speak in softer tones, and in general to be more subdued. At a business meeting, women who talk a lot, raise their voices, or interrupt are apt to be seen as pushy. This places women in management in a double bind: Should they speak out strongly and be considered unfeminine, or remain silent and be considered stupid or submissive?

An individual also expresses the behavior that goes with his personality type and emotional "style." The introvert develops a more distant, aloof style, whereas the extrovert uses expansive postures and gestures. The introvert's muscles are tenser, and his shyness is often mistaken for dislike. The aggressive person develops what psychologists call an "approaching" bodily posture with a forward lean; the reserved person has a withdrawn, "turned away" posture. The proud person is "expansive," standing with an erect or even backward lean of the trunk and head, while the depressed person stands with drooping shoulders, bowed head, and sunken chest. By mid-life, many of these emotional states are etched on the face when it is in "neutral": The happy person will have smile lines around his or her eyes; the unhappy one will have a drooping mouth and tight frown lines.

DETECTING DECEPTION

While some personality traits may be fairly obvious, transient emotional states are more difficult to spot. In business negotiations, it is often hard to tell when somebody is lying or telling only part of the truth.

While there is some truth to the folk belief that a liar "can't look you in the eye" (in one experiment, people who were lying looked at their audience less frequently than when they were telling the truth), experts on facial expression say that the face is not the best clue.

Apparently, the need to detect lying is acute enough to encourage the marketing of what one company advertised in business magazines as "the ultimate truth machine." Unlike the cumbersome lie detector, which must be attached to the subject, the voice-stress analyzer is a little box that sits on your desk. The theory is that lying causes the muscles controlling the vocal cords to tighten, and this machine will pick up these microscopic tremors. However, it may also pick up muscle tightening caused by anxiety.

So far, no method is completely effective, but some people have become considerably skilled in detecting deception without machines. When veteran trial attorney Louis Nizer has a witness on the stand, he watches for changes of behavior when a certain subject is mentioned and then pursues that subject in cross examinations. For example, if a witness puts his hand in front of his mouth every time a sum of money is mentioned, this may be significant. If everything is under control but there is some incongruous nonverbal behavior (for example, the body and face totally relaxed, except for a clenched fist), this can be a distress signal. Voice tremors may be only signs of nervousness, according to Nizer, but if the voice changes pitch or loudness every time a certain subject is mentioned, this signals something.

And eyes are often a giveaway, since they are more difficult to mask than face and body. The eyes have long been associated with revealing emotion. Our language tells us this by the number of words we have for different types of eye contact—the glare, the glance, the darting look, the stare, etc. In the past century, Chinese jade merchants made practical use of the fact that pupils of the eyes dilate when we see something or someone we like. When the merchant saw this response, he could hold out for a higher price. Recent studies by psychologists reveal that not only do men's pupils dilate when looking at an attractive woman (and vice versa) in a photograph, but men will rate the same woman "more attractive" if her pupils are more enlarged. We leave practical application of this information to your own imagination (wearing dark glasses when negotiating a business deal, perhaps?).

Since it takes time to become skilled at nonverbal reading, and since your attention may be fully occupied by the content of a meeting, you might like to adopt a practice used by some law firms. One member of the firm may be conducting the *voire dire* procedure, questioning prospective jurors, while another watches members of the jury panel for revealing body language. Thus, if you negotiate as a team, one person could be assigned to do the talking while the other is assigned to read nonverbal cues.

INTERPRETING SIGNALS THROUGH EYE CONTACT

Since so much nonverbal behavior is complex and difficult to "catch" in motion, it's fortunate that our brains come equipped with the means to interpret for us, especially in one-to-one interactions.

As mentioned in Chapter 2, the left hemisphere of the brain processes intellectual content, while the right monitors the emotive qualities of the interchange. Thus if you pay attention only to the intellectual content of a conversation, you are literally listening with only half a brain.

In a right-handed speaker, the right hand acts like an orchestra conductor, keeping time with gestures to the speech. These gestures are directed to the listener's left visual field/right hemisphere. Meanwhile, the speaker's right ear monitors his own speech, while his left ear keeps track of his listener's interjections. All the while, the listener's right ear decodes the content of the message, while the left ear attends to nonverbal cues.

Eye contact is the chief nonverbal means of signaling whose turn it is to speak when two people are conversing. (One student of the brain has called this eye contact "the invisible parliamentarian" because it signals who takes the floor next.) On film, it's possible to see that, milliseconds before a speaker finishes talking, he looks away from his listener. He then looks back toward the listener and holds the look as he falls silent. At this signal ("I'm finished"), the listener becomes the speaker. If he does not pick up this cue, the pause lengthens into an awkward silence, until one begins to speak or the conversation ends.

Nothing is more disconcerting to a speaker than a listener who refuses to make eye contact. The speaker interprets this as boredom or inattentiveness, and, unless he is unusually persistent or assertive, he will stop speaking and find someone who is more receptive. Another alternative for the speaker is to send signals to an inattentive listener; he may raise his voice, tap his arm, or in some way try to regain his attention.

If you're having difficulties with one-on-one communication—if your talks with people are awkward, end in strained silences, or break off in the middle—you may be violating some of these unwritten eye-contact rules of conversation. If you do most of the talking, you may be failing to give "I'm finished" signals, or you may be rushing in too quickly if your listener doesn't pick up your cues right away.

MIRRORING AND SYNCHRONY

Recently, a team made up of a linguist and several Gestalt psychologists has been teaching businesspeople and others how to detect what is going on in a person's brain by watching his eyes. While the method, which they call "neurolinguistic programming," is still under study, some of the basic ideas about the link between the eyes and the brain's sensory processing are intriguing.

Briefly, when a right-handed person looks up and to the left, he is recalling a visual memory; eyes up and to the right is a new visualization; eyes horizontal, right or left, equals auditory processing; eyes down and to the right means processing kinesthetic input; and eyes down and to the left, signifies internal dialogue, or talking to oneself. The team theorizes that if you know a person's characteristic sensory mode, you will know how to appeal to him. Thus a trial lawyer appearing before a judge who is mainly a visualizer would appeal to him by painting word pictures.

The neurolinguistic programmers also teach business-people how to establish empathy with people they hope to influence by using the behaviors of *mirroring* and *synchrony*. Mirroring is simply the tendency of people in pairs or groups to adopt similar postures, tones of voice, and sometimes dialects and accents. Watch this the next time you lunch with someone. As soon as the first person at the table picks up a fork, the others will mirror this gesture almost immediately. You may also notice at small group meetings that people gradually adopt similar postures. Mirroring enhances rapport.

Synchrony refers to the rhythms of listeners and speakers. One investigator who analyzed films of people conversing found that a person's body literally "dances" to the beat of his or her own speech. All motions follow this rhythmic beat, or synchrony. In *interactional synchrony*, the listener also moves in time to the speaker's voice rhythm. The "lock in" to this rhythm is similar to mirroring and takes place in a flash, like a reflex. Synchrony is weak or nonexistent when a pair is arguing and strong when the two are in agreement. When attention wanders, it is broken.

Neurolinguistic programmers teach business persons to deliberately practice mirroring and synchrony. They claim that the test of your ability is to first achieve synchrony with another, then change your own rhythmic pace and have the other person follow your lead. The object of course is manipulation. Skillful persuaders have always done this intuitively, so you may want to be on your guard against it.

NONVERBAL CUES AS SELF-FULFILLING PROPHECIES

One thing to guard against in reading other people's nonverbal cues is the danger of simply seeing a reflection of yourself and your own attitudes. The Pygmalion Effect, first discovered in an experiment in educational psychology in an elementary school, is an example. Teachers were told that certain students in their classes had been tested, and the results showed that they had great potential. There had been no such tests. Nevertheless, students who had been so identified to the teachers did better than the control group. Since the only difference was the teachers' expectations, the experimenters concluded that the teachers had somehow communicated their expectations to the students nonverbally, and the students had responded. This study opened up all sorts of possibilities, not only in the classroom but wherever results can be influenced by human expectations.

The parallel with a work situation is obvious. If your company has tried something new that isn't working out, it may be that those who were implementing it were saying by the tone of their voice, "This isn't any good" when they gave workers instructions. But you can make the self-fulfilling prophecy work *for* you. If the person presenting a new procedure or policy thinks it will work and gives positive verbal and nonverbal cues, it probably will.

Another self-fulfilling prophecy can be seen in distancing cues. Distances that people establish between themselves can be a function of status (as discussed in Chapter 6), but distancing cues (or "immediacy" cues) are also expressions of likes and dislikes. We instinctively come closer to people we like and stay away from or turn away from people we dislike. The salesperson intuitively uses "liking behavior" to influence potential customers: leaning toward them attentively and smiling, for example. The reverse, however, could happen to you on the job. If, in your encounters with another person, your body is stiff and you tend not to look toward him or speak to him, you may perceive his nonverbal actions toward you as negative, and you may even dislike him. What you may fail to perceive is that your own nonverbal messages are calling forth similar nonverbal messages from him. You are aware of *his* messages but not of your own. (You might try changing your nonverbal behavior toward him and see if his changes, also.)

If you feel that someone dislikes you, that person's nonverbal cues may mean only that *he thinks you don't like him.* Consider the self-fulfilling prophecy of a shy person at a party. He comes expecting not to have a good time, so he stands at a distance from other people, avoiding eye contact because he fears rejection. Ordinarily, a person who wants to approach and speak looks for someone who will respond positively. But the shy person is giving negative signals and is ignored. This reinforces his belief that he's going to have a terrible time. His prophecy is fulfilled, so he prepares for yet another cycle of withdrawal and rejection. Similar dynamics come into play when two people conflict at work, and often such cycles are difficult to break.

PUTTING PEOPLE AT EASE

During a job interview, do you try to help the nervous interviewee with a warm greeting and a genuine display of interest? If you do, an interviewee will usually take his cue from you and will probably show his best qualities and answer your questions openly. If you are stiff and cold, the interviewee will be also.

But aren't there also many everyday situations in which the people who work for you would do better if they felt at ease in your presence? When hearing their complaints or

suggestions, for example, do you give them positive rein-
forcement? Nonverbal signals of listening (head nodding,
eye contact) help, and so does a relaxed, receptive posture.
Uptight postures and gestures or threatening ones, such as
poking or jabbing the finger toward the person will increase
the anxiety he or she feels anyway because of your higher
status and may prevent this person from doing his or her
best. When establishing rapport is especially important,
you might even want to try mirroring or synchrony to help
you feel what the other person is feeling.

To increase your skill at receiving both verbal and nonverbal messages, get in the habit of paying close attention.
Sherlock Holmes used to lecture Dr. Watson on the subject.
If only Watson would use his eyes as he, Holmes, did, he,
too, would see what Holmes saw. ("Elementary, my dear
Watson! The owner of this stick is a young fellow under
thirty, amiable, unambitious, absent-minded and the pos-
sessor of a favorite dog which I should describe as being
larger than a terrier and smaller than a mastiff.")

While you may not aspire to Holmesian feats of
inference-making, your increased awareness of nonverbal
behavior should increase your total listening ability and
your effectiveness as a manager.

Of course, it's possible to be wrong. Nonverbal cues are
best perceived when people are not conscious of sending
them. There you sit, interviewing a job applicant wearing a
pin-striped suit. He leans forward attentively, makes eye
contact with you, and nods in all the right places, but is he
really reliable and trustworthy? Or has he merely read the
right books and applied the right advice to make you think
so? Unfortunately, there is no foolproof way to tell the difference. All you can do is apply your conclusions based on
body language with caution and watch for *clusters of behavior* and *consistency,* not isolated examples.

EXERCISES

1. Practice reading nonverbal communications by
watching a dramatic program (or even a talk show and the

news) with the TV's sound turned off. Study the actors' gestures, facial expressions, and body movements. What can you learn about the emotions and personalities of the characters? How much of the plot can you figure out?

2. Listen to people talk at times when you can be an onlooker and not a participant in the conversation. Tune out the content of the message and try to listen just to the vocal qualities. What emotional qualities do you hear?

3. Can you identify any masks among your co-workers? What kind? Are they worn consistently? Do you ever see them "unmasked?" In what setting or settings?

4. Deliberately change your nonverbal behavior toward someone you dislike. Do you notice any change in this person's behavior toward you or in your feelings for that person?

5. The next time you find yourself in a lengthy conversation, notice whether or not you have adopted a "mirrored" posture. If you have not, try doing so. Do you have any better clue as to how that person feels? Did the conversation go any better?

8

The Corporate Communications Game

A man is known by the company he keeps and a company is known by the men it keeps.

ANON.

PREVIEW

1. Are most of the decisions in your company made at the top, or are they shared throughout the organization?

2. Are there "information leaders" in your company—people who may not have an important title but who seem to know everything that's happening?

3. How does the information flow in your organization? From the top down? How does the information flow within your department?

4. Are there informal information networks in your company? Do you know how to use them successfully?

5. How do you rate the attitudes of people who report to you?

6. To what extent are your top executives concerned with the feelings of the employees? Is there any correlation between their concern (or lack of it) and their managerial effectiveness?

7. How do you feel about the physical surroundings at work? How does the office layout—space, furnishings,

atmosphere—affect the way you interact with others on the job?

8. Is there an active rumor mill in your company? How accurate is it?

All message sending and receiving takes place within a social setting—in this case, the business organization. The setting not only provides a background for the communications process but influences who says what and how and to whom it is said. This chapter examines *institutional* methods of communication and the business organization as a social environment. Since you work and communicate within this environment, you must become more aware of the methods of receiving and sending messages and how they influence your management style. This style is very much dependent on the organization's management style: Who makes the decisions? Who has power, both formal and informal? What are the formal and informal communications networks? By virtue of sheer numbers alone, a business organization is enormously complex. This makes it more difficult, but no less important, for a manager to analyze his or her organization in order to know how to play the corporate game.

ORGANIZATIONAL STRUCTURE: THE HIERARCHY

American corporate structure has traditionally been a hierarchy, symbolized by a pyramid. Its prototype is the military, where a chain of command descends by rank from general to troops. The pyramid, with its ever-smaller and narrower layers, is a good illustration of this kind of hierarchy. The higher you are on the pyramid, the higher your status, and the fewer positions at that level. Each level is separated from the ones above and below it, and there is direct-line, linear reporting from level to level.

Such a hierarchy is even built right into almost every office building in the country. A few top-ranking executives have their offices on the top floor of the building. Each floor then descends by rank; the lowest-ranking and most numerous employees are found on the bottom floor (or even in some cases, underground). In these corporations, "climbing the corporate ladder" is no metaphor. When an individual is promoted, he or she moves up, physically, floor by floor, each climb in office location getting closer and closer to the executive suite at the top of the building.

The organizational pyramid makes no bones about the way it distinguishes the Indians from the chiefs. Just to make sure, some organizations use titles to differentiate each level of status, and some even attach a numbering system to each title. Thus a first-line supervisor may be at Level 1. Salary and benefits would be scaled according to rank and number. Employees may not wear stars and bars to indicate rank, but they have no doubt where they stand. Status is symbolized not by stripes on their sleeves but by dress and office location, design, and furnishings.

However, dissatisfaction with the rigidity of the hierarchy has led to alternative organizational structures within the last decade or so. These are functionally based, rather than status-oriented structures, with workers divided into teams rather than ranks. A flattened rather than a tall organizational structure encourages more employee participation in an effort to motivate them to become more productive. Often, profit sharing and incentive plans accompany flat structure/project-team types of organizations. These are largely experimental, but they may be prototypes of the future.

COMMUNICATING IN THE HIERARCHY

Most of us still work in hierarchical organizations, and their structure defines the formal lines of communication that we must work with (or against). People who have worked in a hierarchical organization for any length of time will tell you that the strongest flow of information is in one direction—downward. The reason is simple: Your life on the job depends on understanding the messages from above. When an upper level "sends," you must be ready to receive.

However, since decision-making at the top of the pyramid is dependent upon information from below, many companies actively seek to improve upward communication. This isn't easy, for the larger the company, the more difficult it is to send a message up the line. This is true for several reasons. First of all, top managers generally feel that it is less important to listen to their subordinates than to their superiors. Not listening can be used as a status symbol. It is traditional for the person of higher status to talk and the lower status to listen. A superior can reinforce his status in his own eyes and the eyes of subordinates by interrupting them, changing the subject, and in general making it hard for them to get their messages through. Secondly, the "taller" the structure of the organization, the more levels the message must pass through to reach the top. Most organizations of any size have an active "filtering system" that acts to block or alter messages from below. The filtering system is usually most active at middle-management levels. It interferes with the flow of communications, making it much easier for information to travel downward through the filter than upward.

Executives and higher-level managers who remain unaware of the filtering process probably lose touch with the lower levels of their organizations. They may contract a major organizational disease: *executive isolation.* An organization suffering from this malady is in big trouble. The flow of communication is blocked and somehow must be reopened, or the organization will die. W. T. Grant Company, for example, which in 1975 experienced the biggest retailing failure ever, continued to open new stores while its old ones were losing money. New York headquarters either didn't know or didn't care to know what was going on in the field, and when new management tried to respond, it was too late.

In organizations where workers are unionized, a type of "end run" can be made around the blockage. Most managers agree that the union often receives information from the top more quickly than those at lower management levels. First-line supervisors often complain about this in statements such as, "If I want to know what's going on in the company, I ask my workers, not my boss." This happens because of top management's tendency to check out a new policy or major decision early with the union to avoid violating the current contractual agreement. While this procedure is logical, it means that management has told the union first, which makes the workers privy to the information before most of their own managers are. It represents, to the first-line supervisor, an erosion of power and authority, and understandably enough, it's thoroughly resented.

Lateral communication, the exchange of information among those of relatively equal status in the hierarchy, also occurs within an organization. It is usually more effective than upward communication, but not as effective as downward flow because of the competition between employees on the same rungs of the organizational ladder. The very people who have the greatest opportunity and the greatest need to communicate (because they work together on a daily basis) often have the least motivation to do so. After all, you don't want to give away valuable information if you're not certain your co-workers will reciprocate. Ideally, the effective manager should practice active listening on *every* level of his organization. But in reality, the hierarchical structure makes this difficult. No matter how sharp your listening skills, the organization structure itself tends to block your use of them. Often people learn more from rumors than from official announcements.

OFFICE RUMORS AS COMMUNICATION

Rumors seem to be as much a part of the furnishings of an organization as the desks and chairs. In fact, they play a large part in group life. They are a means by which people cope with what they can't or won't understand, or with whatever is frightening them. Since people usually fear what they don't understand, often the two causes of rumor are one. Whatever is threatening or not understood creates anxiety; rumor dispels anxiety by seeming to explain things.

One of the strange aspects of rumor is that even an explanation that predicts some kind of disaster is preferred to no explanation at all. During the accident at The Three Mile Island nuclear power plant in Pennsylvania in 1979, rumors were flying that a nuclear meltdown was imminent. Whenever the public is alarmed, officials take to the airwaves to deny the rumors and give the "true" version. Whether or not they will be believed depends on the officials' current credibility with the public. If the public believes that these officials have lied to them in the past, it reasons that they are likely to do so again and it will refuse to believe their version.

The same holds true within the business organization. Whenever some change is in the air, the future becomes clouded. The change will undoubtedly affect people's jobs, but they don't know how. This uncertainty creates anxiety, so the rumor mills grind overtime. Whether or not the employees believe the organization's attempts to dispel the rumor depends on top management's record of credibility with employees. If it is low, no amount of official denying will dispel the rumors.

However, potential change and the organization's credibility isn't the only factor in the persistence and spread of rumors. Anxious individuals tend to believe and spread rumors much more readily than calm ones. In times of economic uncertainty, a great many employees are likely to be anxious and, therefore, rumor-prone. Combine large numbers of anxious people in an organization with a low-credibility management and you have the perfect climate for rumors. Rumors are like mushrooms; they grow best in the dark. An organization that has an atmosphere of super-secrecy, where all planning is very hush-hush and nobody is allowed to talk until the "president makes the official announcement," will have a flourishing rumor industry within its corridors.

Anything that touches people's lives will give rise to rumors, but most rumors in organizations are relatively short-lived: from the time a new boss takes over until people get to know him and know what to expect; from the time a new job is created until somebody fills it; from the time a move is contemplated until it actually takes place. If management vacillates or a decision is delayed, rumors will last that much longer. When something is actually happening rather than being anticipated, interest in rumors dies—until next time.

Rumors are often self-serving, reinforcing people's vanities and prejudices. When a promotion is in the offing, not everyone will make it, so it's more comforting to blame equal opportunity laws: "He only got the job because he's black" or ". . . because she's a woman" is easier to accept than the idea that he or she is more competent.

Real life is often tentative, ambiguous, and dull; rumors enliven the workaday world. Unlike real life, rumors have well-defined plots. They improve on real life by assigning motives to the characters, embellishing the actions and, frequently, by bringing the story to completion. It's much more dramatic to hear that Judy Jenkins lost her job because Hattie Hightower (who's sleeping with her boss) wanted her out, than because poor Judy was incompetent.

GOLF WITH THE BOSS:
INFORMAL NETWORKS

People like to *know,* and in the absence of authoritative information, they will seek out other sources, particularly about decisions that will directly affect their own work. *The more an organization insists on using formal lines of reporting, the greater the likelihood that an informal communication network will emerge.*

When organizations adhere strictly to formal lines, information often reaches employees too little and too late. Just as the Navy has its scuttlebutt, every organization has its grapevine. When a particular grapevine becomes reliable, it then functions as an informal informational network. One of the key differences between formal and informal communications networks is that the formal follows the hierarchical structure, while the informal does not.

For many reasons, people within an organization have friends on different levels of the hierarchy. A middle manager, particularly one who has spent many years in an organization, may have friends on several levels above and below. He or she has crossed paths over the years with a variety of individuals. Perhaps they have worked together and then were promoted or moved on, but they still maintain some channels of communication with each other. Such an interconnecting chain can send messages through an organization with lightning speed.

A manager with multiple sources of information has a great advantage in terms of information power. Eventually, as people are added to the group he's in touch with, a viable second communication network is formed, and this can be a powerful force in an organization. There are three basic requirements for a solid informal network:

1. It should be able to tap into employees on all levels of the organization. (At least one member must be part of the top-management team.)
2. It is, unlike the formal network, built on an attitude of personal trust. Thus it has a more solid foundation than the formal network. In order to keep going, there must be a shared agreement within the network that each member will be responsible for passing on information quickly and accurately.
3. It does not spread "rumors." It's information is primarily factual.

The larger and more hierarchical your organization, the stronger the possibility that an informal network is alive and functioning within it. For years, skillful managers have used these informal systems to their advantage. They just "happen" to know things before they occur, or they make good "guesses" about what's going on. How? They've had advance warning. That's exactly what an informal communication network is: an early warning system.

In fact, more than one informal network may exist within the same organization. Several may be broad and multi-level: the operating vice-president and all of his former plant personnel now scattered throughout the company, for instance, or that social clique that does indeed play golf with the president. In addition, often smaller informal networks operate within individual departments and sections. It may be useful for a manager to be able to tap into more than one network in order to receive different types of information.

A note of caution. Informal networks have been in existence for a long time. In fact, people who were once managers may be top executives now because they tapped into the right informal networks. Not only may they be aware of the networks' existence, but they may sometimes use the networks to test their organization. Occasionally, purposefully incorrect information is sent just to get a reaction in a problem situation. Thus you must be cautious and analytical about the information that you pass on.

The network should never be used to gain status. Although you may gain temporarily, you risk losing credibility if the information is incorrect. These networks would quickly lose their effectiveness if they turned into rumor mills. People are often subtly dropped from informal networks because they passed on information in order to make themselves look good (e.g., by seeming "in the know" or "knowing people in high places.")

It is characteristic of a powerful informal network that it is the information flow, not the sender, that's important. Informal networks work best when the higher-level sources of the information are never revealed and when the information is accurate.

OFFICE TURFS

All humans have places and possessions that they regard as "theirs," even if they are not the legal owners. Whether it's a church pew or a park bench, anyone who sits in the same seat regularly comes to think of it as his or hers. The cook's kitchen, Archie Bunker's chair, the gang's back alley, the teacher's classroom, the home team's playing field are all examples of "turfs." A work group may take over a break room by occupying and using it regularly so that other groups come to think of it as "theirs," not "ours."

Robert Sommer, a researcher who devoted a great deal of time to the study of dominance and territoriality in mental institutions, found that each hospital had a well-established dominance hierarchy, each with its assigned space. Not only patients, but nurses and attendants were uncomfortable when Sommer, a doctor, sat down next to a patient in the day room. That was the patients' space, just as the nurses' stations belonged to the nurses.

A corner office may have become a "power position" (to quote Michael Korda) because corner positions are best for seeing what goes on and thus are easiest to defend. Where, for instance, would you sit in a large restaurant if you wanted to see who entered and left? Probably at a corner table with your back to the wall, facing the entrance. When seated at a table, the corner position is the easiest to defend from intruders.

A pair of social scientists have distinguished four types of territories in human societies:

1. Public, with free access, such as parks, streets, lobbies.
2. Home territories, with public access controlled by a group, such as a local bar or hangout, some workplace lunchrooms.
3. Interactional, a setting for people to interact socially, such as a break room, lounge.
4. Personal, controlled by an individual, such as a desk or private room or office.

Some spaces may serve a dual purpose. For example, two people in an elevator (public) may be engaged in an interchange of information (interactional). A company's real commitment to communication often can be gauged by the amount of space it makes available for interaction; if there is not enough space, public areas will be pressed into service—halls, elevators, restrooms.

The need for neutral or interactional space is often felt most acutely when differences need to be ironed out or policies negotiated, since people acting within their home territories have a built-in advantage (as the home team does in ball games). Why else does your boss call you into *his* office for a talk? Social scientists who wanted to put this idea to the test had student lawyers, one of the pair representing the prosecutor and one representing a defendant, negotiate a plea bargain in their respective dormitory rooms to see if the student was able to get better terms for his client when in his own dormitory. He was.

Another test of a company's people-orientation is how it handles the need for privacy. When people are crowded together and can't get away from each other, they will often get away by "cocooning," or retreating into themselves. Needless to say, this behavior discourages informal communications. Where do you go when you need to withdraw and think—away from ringing phones and constant interruption from other people? Like harried mothers of young children, some managers have literally nowhere to go to get away from their charges except the restroom.

Does your company permit employees to have personal territory that they control, such as a desk or wall space that they can personalize with pictures, plants, signs, or posters? (The company that forbids this is telling its people something—that this space is not really theirs.) Do employees have privacy, or are all the desks out in the open so that you have to counsel a worker in full view (and possibly hearing) of everyone else? Even if no one else can hear, the fear of the possibility of being overheard will stifle communication.

The open office in which every desk can be seen at once, rather than being democratic, is the exact opposite. An autocratic management that doesn't trust its employees has arranged to have them watched. Even in open offices, people will still stake out individual and group territories, but the markers will be more subtle. A softened plan, the office "landscape" with movable partitions and greenery, gives lower-echelon people privacy, but sometimes takes it away from middle managers and supervisors, who resent it.

What Sommer calls "hard architecture"—the bureaucratic or hierarchical building—is one in which everything has its place; people as well as things are kept apart. It attempts to ensure that all interactions will follow strictly prescribed patterns by restricting the movement of people, "keeping them in their place." Within it, communication is discouraged, except the messages that come down from the top through "correct channels."

MANAGEMENT STYLES: WHAT MAKES A WINNING TEAM?

Most employees have at least some negative feelings about hierarchical corporate structures—and they cope with these feelings in various ways. (The formation of informal information networks is one type of coping behavior.) These negative feelings are occasioned mainly by the way managers treat their employees. In short, by management styles.

Most writers on the subject divide management styles predominantly into *task-oriented* or *people-oriented.* These in turn relate to the two categories of behavior associated with the manager's job: (1) task behaviors, aimed at turning out a product or service, and (2) people behaviors, aimed at building healthy worker/boss relationships.

Managers who are strongly task-oriented are generally more concerned with getting the work out, going by the book, and measuring success by the numbers. People-oriented managers, on the other hand, tend to be less concerned with numbers and results, use "the book" more as a general guideline, and stress the development of people.

Managers veer toward one direction or the other based on the way they view the requirements of the job and the requirements of the pervading style of the organization. In other words, not only do individuals have distinct, identifiable management styles, but so do departments, divisions, and entire organizations. Obviously, the pervading styles of the organization directly influence the individual's style. *Problems arise when an individual's style is in conflict with that of the organization.*

Are you a task-oriented or a people-oriented manager? How did you get that way? Can you tell from your organization's style how your own style developed and perhaps why you are sometimes forced to manage in ways that make you uncomfortable?

Each organization is a system with its own rules, checks and balances, and priorities that govern the way the company functions. In other words, each organization has its own style. Our discussion of corporate style is an adaptation of the "four-system theory" of Rensis Likert and Associates of the Institute of Social Research in Ann Arbor, Michigan.

System 1 is just about identical with the hierarchical military model that developed out of 19th-century needs. At the other end of the scale is System 4, which has no real counterpart (or very few) in today's business world. Systems 1 and 2 cover the majority of all companies today, and we will briefly describe System 4 as an instructive comparison. Each system also has its own type of managerial office layout.

System 1 Organizations

1. High task and production orientation.
2. Devaluing of the workers and the needs of the people.
3. Strong emphasis on rules and regulations.
4. Use of punishment, threats, and fear to make people produce.
5. Strong maintenance of the hierarchical structure and direct-line reporting.
6. Decision-making and vital information hoarded at the top.
7. Communication almost exclusively downward.

8. Authoritarian and autocratic leadership style starting at the executive level and copied throughout the organization.

System 1 organizations seem to ignore the needs of people and the organization's responsibility to its workers. Organizations that continue to operate this way are probably much less productive than other types. Often, they are characterized by a high degree of white-collar turnover, low productivity, strong unions, strong informal informational networks, large amounts of overtime, and inadequate break rooms and leisure-time facilities. The average age of employees is over 40, and there are few (if any) minorities or women in the managerial ranks.

Although System 1 organizations break with most modern ideas about how organizations should be operated, it appears that at least *one-third* of American companies are closer to System 1 than to any of the others. Part of the reason for this is simply inertia: The larger the organization, the more deeply embedded is the organizational style.

Even in less rigid organizations, there are pockets of the System 1 style—certain departments, certain job functions, certain members of top management who are still living in the "good old days." They may produce some short-term results, but they will be largely unsuccessful in the long run. These System 1 pockets must either adapt to new modes or decline.

System 2 Organizations

1. Attempt to soften the emphasis on product and task-orientation and promote people-orientation.
2. Strong emphasis on improving working conditions, salary, and benefits; addition of "human relations" training so that managers can understand the needs of employees.
3. Maintenance of rules, yet selective "bending" occurs.
4. Widespread manipulation of employees through use of inducements such as promised advancement and

glossy "public relations" recognition of good performance.

5. Maintenance of hierarchy, but with increased knowledge and ability of top management to tap into informal networks.

6. Decision-making still primarily at the top, but some minor decisions delegated downward (often characterized by titular department heads with responsibility but little authority).

7. Communication flow primarily downward with some new projects introduced to encourage some upward flow.

8. Leadership style quasi-democratic with emphasis on paternalism.

As organizations become more concerned with their employees—sometimes as a result of the pressure of unions or government agencies—some respond by moving toward a System 2 approach. However, unless you're fairly high up, System 2 is not much better to work in than System 1. At least System 1 is direct, honest, and standardized; if you break the rules, you're punished, and that's that. But System 2 organizations often cajole their employees into believing that they have a say in their work lives, when in reality they don't.

A typical example of System 2 behavior is placing individualized thermostats in every department. Since, of course, no two people can agree on a comfortable temperature, the wall thermostats are dummies. The real thermostats are hidden in the ceiling and centrally controlled.

Can a new carpet on the floor and increased medical and dental benefits buy happiness? Perhaps temporarily. Perhaps even some of the time for some of the people. At least with higher incomes and benefits, workers are freer to pursue happiness *outside* the job. But they may be no happier from 9 to 5 than the System 1 employee.

You can probably click off numbers of personal acquaintances and co-workers who fit into the following description of an average employee in a System 2 organization:

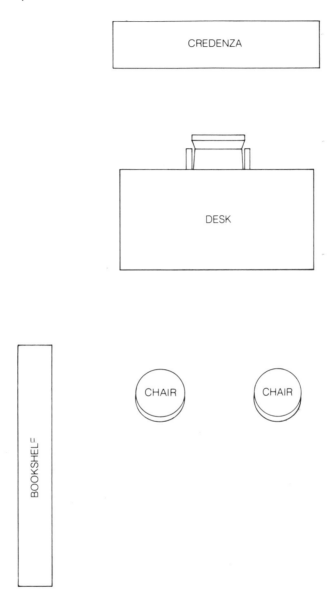

System 1 office layout: Desk is in the central position in the room. Guest chairs are positioned across from the desk and at some distance from it. Environment is generally sterile and the furniture quality and style is determined by position in the hierarchy.

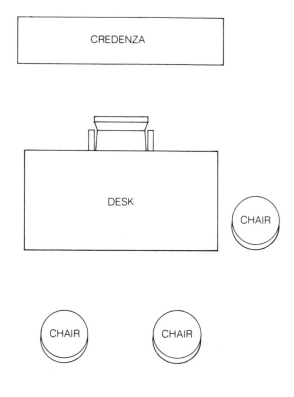

System 2 office layout: Desk is slightly off center but still the predominant piece. Guest chairs are closer to the boss and one is adjacent to him. Environment remains generally sterile with a few "softeners" such as plants and wall hangings.

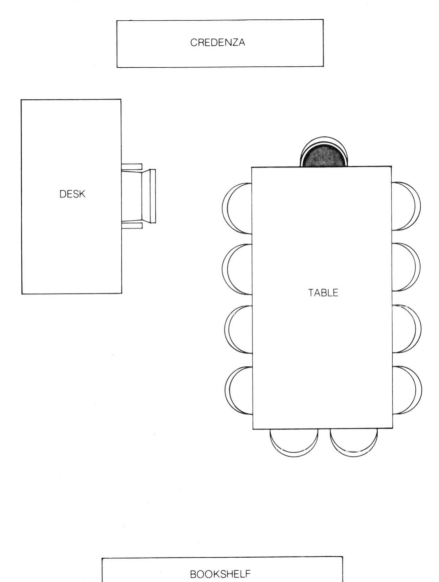

System 3 office layout: Desk is moved out of central focal position. Table is added, but it is generally a rectangular shape. The boss usually sits at position of authority at the table. Decorations will be similar to System 2.

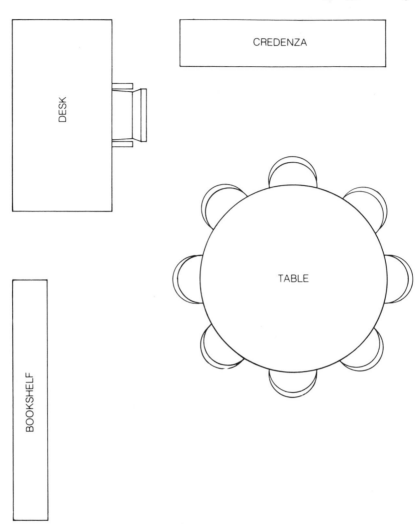

System 4 office layout: Desk is in the most non-predominant position in the room. The boss's back is to the door, indicating trust. Table is circular, encouraging equal participation. The arrangement of chairs forces the boss to converse around the table or, if he is seated at the desk, to turn and face the table.

Good Old Joe

Joe has been working for XYZ Manufacturing for ten years. He's thirty-five years old and has been a second-line supply manager for four years. He topped out in the salary range last year and takes home a comfortable salary of $21,000, in addition to the full insurance benefits provided by the company. He's even invested in the stock plan and now feels that he owns a piece of XYZ.

Joe isn't an outstanding manager, but he treats his co-workers well. They meet most of the deadlines and generally provide a fair day's work for a fair day's pay. Joe's boss keeps encouraging him to "hang in there," his time for a promotion will come. But it's beginning to look less promising.

About a year ago Joe and his wife bought a sailboat with some money she had inherited, and now they take their two children out almost every weekend. Joe will also assume the presidency of his local Rotary Club next fall, he coaches one of the Little League baseball teams, and he's a valued member of the junior high school Parent Advisory Board.

He even mentioned to his wife that he was considering going into a second business with a friend of his. It wouldn't take much time, and after all, there's still some of that inheritance left. Besides, the family car will hold up for another year or two.

Does this example ring a bell? Would you promote Joe? How would you manage him? (Are *you* by any chance Joe?) He's obviously got some talent that is untapped at XYZ and that he's redirected into other, outside activities.

This situation is a common one in American corporate life today, especially in System 2 organizations. Certainly the working conditions and salaries are great, but the real motivators are still missing—the excitement of doing interesting and challenging work, of growing and learning and "stretching" oneself to do even better.

System 3 Organizations

1. Marked increase in concern for employees.
2. Strong emphasis on evaluating the potential and interest of all employees so that they can be properly placed in interesting and challenging work; increased

opportunities for movement within the organization, with both upward and lateral moves based on career paths designed by employees and assessment centers.

3. Company policy and rules used more as general guidelines.
4. Increased involvement of employees in decision-making and increased delegation of authority and responsibility.
5. General "softening" of the hierarchical structure, lessening of middle-management ranks, and emergence of project "teams" assigned to temporary job functions.
6. Decision-making pushed down to levels where the most information is available.
7. Strong *upward* flow of communication through attitude surveys, upward communication programs, viable suggestion plans, visible movement of top management among worker ranks in the field.
8. "Participative" leadership style, with employees encouraged to give input into decisions that will directly affect their jobs.

Although most organizations operate under System 2, some departments or pockets within them seem to approach the more people-oriented structures of System 3. System 3 is an attempt to adapt the corporate structure to tap the wealth of resources contained in its employees— because the productivity of the company's work force depends on it. A few isolated examples exist of whole companies operating under System 3. Harwood Manufacturing Company of Marion, Virginia, which has been frequently cited in recent management literature, began this system thirty years ago and has enjoyed increased growth and productivity ever since.

System 4: The Organization of the Future

1. Negation of the hierarchical structure; strong "team" management used.
2. Emphasis on *functional management,* rather than

tasks or people. Work organized by functions and projects which are constantly changing as the market and employees change.

3. Division of labor from boss/subordinates (management and workers) to project "teams" with a group of "equals" assigned to complete a project.
4. Emergence of the concept of "matrix teams." Individual jobs are determined by assignments to several different functional teams. An individual may work on several teams at one time.
5. High value is placed on worker autonomy and initiative: the individual employee charts his/her own "career path," sets his/her own goals, and becomes a full partner in decisions which result from project "teams."
6. Standardized corporate rules and policy are minimal. Employees set their own standards, operate on flexible hours, evaluate team members' contributions to the effort, share in the profits of the organization on the basis of the contribution of their team.
7. Decision-making is relatively equally shared throughout the organization. Top management's function is largely one of long-range planning for the corporation as a whole.
8. Communication flow within the organization is excellent, particularly laterally. Due to the elimination of pyramid concepts, upward and downward communication are much less applicable.

CHANGING YOUR ORGANIZATION'S STYLE

Which office-arrangement diagram is most like your own? Do you like it? Is it making you more effective or hindering you? Which of the organizational systems is your company like?

If System 4 sounds ideal, it's still a long way off for most of us. How can we get there, assuming that we want to? Some changes must be initiated by top management, but there are other changes that you could make to bring about a healthier work environment.

1. *Know what your employees need and want.* The desires of most of today's employees were aptly summed up in a 1973 *Work in America* article:

What the workers want most, as more than 200 studies in the past 20 years show, is to become masters of their immediate environments and to feel that their work and they themselves are important—the twin ingredients of self-esteem. Workers recognize that some of the dirty jobs can be transformed only into merely tolerable, but the most oppressive features of work are felt to be meaningless tasks, constant supervision and coercion, lack of variety, monotony, and isolation—all avoidable. An increasing number of workers want more autonomy in tackling their tasks, greater opportunity for increasing their skills, rewards that are directly connected to the intrinsic aspects of work, and greater participation in the design of work and formulation of their tasks.

2. *Listen to the ideas and input of employees* on all levels in order to encourage the upward flow of communications. What can you do to open the channels above you? If it is within your power, insist that executives get out of the office and start getting to know the work force. Have them visit areas over which they have no authority. If you use attitude surveys, report the findings to employees honestly and ask *them* for solutions to the problems identified.

3. *Encourage lateral communication* by working more closely with your own colleagues. Find ways to get people together informally and to promote more interchanges of ideas. Are there people on your own level whom you have been excluding, such as minorities and women? Their input could be valuable.

4. *Stop believing that power and status are derived from title and position.* Real power is earned by the esteem of people who trust and respect you, as you trust and respect them. Start practicing the Golden Rule.

5. *Look hard at the real needs of people.* Don't attempt to placate employees with new carpeting and other "improvements." Is the work you ask them to do mundane, routine, boring? Can any jobs be restructured? Can some of your own tasks be delegated? Can you include them in more decision-making? Can any people who are no longer challenged by their jobs be moved laterally?

6. *Be receptive to new ideas and change.* Place high value on education and individual growth for yourself and your employees. Try to encourage your co-workers and your company to look for and adopt new ideas, and you do the same.

7. *Take a close look at your organizational structure.* Are there departments reporting to you that are top heavy or individuals performing functions that are no longer needed? Analyze functions to be performed rather than departments to be staffed. If it is within your power, consider project teams. Does the space you are using help or hinder the changes you want to make? Could you make the physical setting more responsive to yours and other people's needs?

This chapter, and the exercises below, provide a means of analyzing your and your company's management styles. Once your analysis is complete, you may find a discrepancy between your own management style and that of your organization. You may want to adjust, or you may decide to make some changes within your own areas of responsibility.

EXERCISES

1. Make a drawing of your organization's structure from the president down through the employees according to job titles. (Your personnel department may have a list.) Which is the structure more like—the traditional pyramid-type hierarchy or the flatter, project team approach?

2. Analyze the *downward* communication flow in your organization as follows:

    a. Take the organizational chart that you just made and see how many *names* you can fill in. Did you include all executives and everyone to and including your own level? How many could you identify by name below you? Were you more familiar with certain departments?

    b. In order to check the effectiveness of your company's downward flow, identify an announcement of some importance that was made within the last month. Next, identify the people on the lower levels whom you have occasion to talk to. The next time you see them, ask them if they know about this announcement. See if they fully understand it.

    c. In order to "check yourself," do the same with your own direct reports to subordinates. Choose something you told them about a month ago, and see if they got it.

3. Analyze the *upward* communication flow:

    a. Choose an issue, project, or report that you would like to bring to the attention of your executive(s). What form of communication would you choose? How would you know if you were successful?

    b. Identify something that one of the people who report to you has done that you feel is excellent. Devise a method of bringing it to the attention of your top executives. See how successful it is. Remember, good management involves getting appropriate recognition for the performance of employees.

4. To analyze the *lateral* communication flow:

    a. Select a few key people in positions equivalent to your own (peer level) and pick a piece of new, interesting information to pass on to them. See where the information travels, how fast, and with what accuracy. Try to determine what path it took—who added to it, changed it, and so forth. Did it get to any higher-level managers or executives? If so, what was its route?

    b. The exercise for lateral communication flow is also

a good one for determining the informal communication network. Who was involved in the spread of the information? Could you have predicted it? Do these people have an informal network in your company? If so, can you tap into it and use it to your advantage again?

5. Using your original organizational chart, play a game of "connect the dots," by connecting the names that you feel form an informal communication network in your company. Is there more than one? If so, use more than one color and identify as many as you can. See how far *up* and how far *down* each goes within the organization.

6. Answer the following questions about your company, about your department, and about the group you supervise:

Do most people seem concerned with just keeping their jobs?

Do most people enjoy their work and think that it is interesting and challenging?

When people do an outstanding job, are they usually rewarded with money, better working conditions, or a day off? Is your own boss told when one of your people does an outstanding job?

Is there any real opportunity to move up, to get a promotion?

Is management generally more concerned with getting the work out than with the contributions and needs of the individual employees?

Are people less concerned with good teamwork and more with making themselves look good?

Is the leadership fairly traditional? Is most of the decision-making done at the top?

Is it difficult for someone to get a message to a manager or executive? Can your staff speak freely with you?

7. If you have identified some management or communication problems in your company or department, is there anything *you* could do to correct them? The place to start is with your own work group. Ask the people who report to you for their ideas. Talk with your boss and get advice. The changes you make for the better will not only help you and your people, but the entire company!

9

Getting Your Message Across

There are two types of conversation: "when you speak and when you listen to yourself speak."
JOHN FOWLES, *Daniel Martin*

PREVIEW

1. Are there some people who seem to have more difficulty understanding you than others? Do you know why?

2. When you are called to your boss's office, do you ever get uptight because you feel you won't present yourself well?

3. Have you ever had the feeling that your boss says things just to impress you with how much he knows? Do you ever do the same to your co-workers?

4. In a conversation, are you often more concerned about how the other person sees you than with what you are trying to convey?

5. Do you feel that you sometimes appear to be inarticulate to others? Do you know why?

6. When asking a question, do you ever find your tone of voice conveys impatience unintentionally?

7. When you give instructions to someone, does he or she ever do the opposite of what you said? Who do you blame?

8. Have you ever planned the way in which you will give instructions? Do you think this would be a good idea?

Until now, the role of the *receiver* of the communication has been emphasized: listening to the message, reading nonverbal cues, and understanding formal and informal communication networks in business situations. However, the role of the *sender* of the communication is equally vital because the sender presents the matrix of ideas that will be responded to, interpreted, and acted upon. The two crucial communication principles for the sender are to solicit feedback and to receiver-orient the message. The power of the message is directly dependent on how well it is oriented to the receiver. The most important way to be persuasive is to put your messages to the receiver in ways that he or she can understand.

In old-style management, the need to please the boss "or else" usually made all other forms of persuasion unnecessary. But management by coercion is no longer effective. An employee must feel that an order or decision is fair before he or she will take action. That means if you want to persuade others to see something *your* way, you must first see it *their* way.

Instead of using the word *persuasion*, it may be helpful to think of message-sending as selling. As the sender, you must sell yourself, your point of view, and your ideas to the receiver. This raises a paradoxical problem: A salesperson has a strong ego, yet in order to succeed, he or she must concentrate on the customer's needs. This is also true of effective message-sending in business situations: The manager has ideas, strategies, and instructions to communicate, but first he must envision the communication from the receiver's point of view.

Successful communication means that the receiver understands the message in the same way that the sender intended it. In this chapter, we will examine six types of sender responsibilities, concentrating on the attitudes and skills needed to make messages more receiver-oriented and to use language more effectively.

DEVELOPING SENDING SKILLS

To develop sending skills, the sender must recognize and accept these responsibilities:

S   et the scene.
E   nunciate clearly.
N   otify the receiver on important points.
D   emand feedback.
E   liminate the unnecessary.
R   eceiver-orient the message.

Let's take a closer look at these seven responsibilities and expand them a bit.

Set the Scene

The first step in setting the scene for successful communication is to make sure you are clear about your message and your reasons for sending it. What do you want to accomplish? Do you want the receiver to learn, to act, or to develop a particular attitude, or all three? You're more likely to reach your objective if you are organized from the beginning.

Choose a time to present the message when the receiver will be most able to use his good listening skills and be most receptive. For example, if he's not a "morning person," don't hit him at 8:05 A.M., before he's had his coffee. And don't initiate an important discussion when the receiver is recovering from jet lag or coming down with the flu.

An appropriate setting is also important. If your conversation will be lengthy and important, find a quiet setting where you won't be interrupted by visitors or phone calls. And consider the receiver's feelings about the environment: Giving a performance appraisal in the local pub obviously is not appropriate.

Before you plunge into your message encourage the receiver to ask questions, to respond, and most important, to let you know whenever he or she doesn't understand. This is probably the most important step in setting the scene. You can make it or break it in these early minutes.

Enunciate Clearly

A good message can fail if you slur words or speak too softly. Your listeners will think you don't really want to talk to them. Your voice delivery is an important part of the communication. Speak distinctly. Many people have a tendency to drop the final consonants from words or to swallow parts of the ends of words, phrases, or sentences (e.g., "Whadayamean?" instead of "What do you mean?"). Be sure you can pronounce words correctly. All of us have far more words in our reading vocabularies than in our speaking vocabularies, and you may mispronounce a word that you've seen only in print. Either look up the word beforehand or don't use it.

Keep your volume appropriate and use voice inflections. Speaking too softly or too loudly for the environment you're in will distract from your message. Vary your volume to maintain attention, and clue the receiver as to what's most important. Most people increase their volume to emphasize a point, but a "softer" emphasis can be equally effective. Vary your pitch, too. No one likes to listen to a monotone. Pitch changes will clue the listener as to what's important and will sustain attention. It also pays to vary your speaking rate. Some people speak so rapidly that you can't keep up or so slowly that your mind wanders between every phrase. The key is variety.

Above all, *put energy into your delivery.* Be animated and energetic about your message. This goes a long way toward motivating your receiver. If *you* sound bored, why should your listener be interested?

Notify the Receiver on Important Points

The possibility of being misunderstood is higher if the receiver has to take time to absorb the parts of the message with no warning. The sender can minimize this by doing the following:

1. Let the receiver know about how much *time* you think the conversation will take so he or she will be mentally prepared. (Be sure to take into account time needed for responses and questions.) Statements like "This should take about fifteen minutes" are helpful. Always be specific: "A few minutes" can mean anything.

2. Tell the receiver right away what the *topic* of the conversation will be. Don't try to disguise it, particularly if it may be unpleasant. (But don't bludgeon him with it either.)

3. Keep the receiver informed about *where you are* in the message. Tell him how many points you intend to make, which point you are now making, and how many more there will be. This will help your receiver to organize his listening and will let him know that you've organized your own thinking. If possible, *enumerate* ("I want to tell you three things") or give *spatial or temporal clues* ("This happened yesterday at 4 P.M. in the cafeteria").

4. Let the receiver know the importance of each statement, either verbally ("Now this next part is the real meat of it") or through gesture, facial expression, or voice cues.

Demand Feedback

Demand is a strong word. If you have set a comfortable atmosphere for the conversation, you may need only to solicit feedback or simply wait for it. This can be done verbally ("Stop me any time you have a question") or by pausing between statements and looking expectantly at your receiver. Receiving feedback is the *only* way you can assure yourself that you're being understood. Example:

YOU: Now I want you to look at this operation very critically . . . .

RECEIVER [*Much later*]:   Come to think of it, I did find a lot that could stand improvement in the way they were

. . . .

YOU [*To yourself*]: Omigosh, when I said "critical" he thought that I meant to criticize. I'd better correct this misconception. [*Out loud*]: Let's not forget what's right with the operation, too. When I said I wanted you to look at it critically, I really meant that I wanted you to be very analytical because . . . .

And when you solicit feedback, you must listen actively to it to prevent misinterpretations by both parties.

Some receivers give nonverbal feedback by nodding affirmatively or smiling. If you know the person well, this may be enough. However, too often it is not enough. If your message is important, you should solicit *verbal* feedback. But there's a trick to doing this effectively. If you ask, "Do you understand what I'm saying?" The receiver's options are limited to yes or no. Most people will reply affirmatively when asked by a superior. (Nobody wants to appear stupid.) You must ask questions that will allow the receiver to translate your message into a response. Ask questions such as "What will this mean to your operation?" or "What will you do about this?" You may even ask a perceptual-check question, such as "Just to be sure we're clear, what does this mean to you?" If distortions appear in the receiver's explanation, you can quickly correct them.

Feedback is the key to successful communication. Start asking for it and then *wait* until it comes. Exercise some patience. It may take awhile if your people aren't used to responding, but the wait will be worth it.

Eliminate the Unnecessary

Most people use 30 percent more words than necessary to express ideas. The acronym KISS (Keep It Simple, Stupid) could well mean Keep It *Short* and Simple. If you feel that you have not said enough, wait, solicit feedback, and then elucidate if necessary. Too often, by saying too much, we distort the real message and confuse the listener. The important points are lost amid too many unimportant words.

Eliminate unnecessary topics of conversation as well as unnecessary words. If you have done a good job of setting the scene, you should be able to get right to the point without having to talk all around it first.

Receiver-Orient the Message

In *The Language and Thought of the Child*, the well-known psychologist Jean Piaget says: "[the child] talks either for himself or for the pleasure of associating anyone who happens to be there with the activity of the moment. This talk is *ego-centric*, partly because the child speaks only about himself, but chiefly because *he does not attempt to place himself at the point of view of his hearer . . . .* He feels no desire to influence his hearers nor to tell them anything" [Emphasis added].

Occasionally, people become stuck at this immature level. They are the chatterers and the bores, who are interested only in themselves. Everyone reverts to this level from time to time because we all like to talk about ourselves (which is why good listeners are popular—it's so flattering), but monologues are essentially self-indulgent. Often, we speak "to hear ourselves talk." This really cuts out the receiver entirely and we deliver a *sender-oriented* message, for our benefit, not the listeners.

Receiver-orientation is an *attitude* as well as a set of skills. It is the attitude that we wish to emphasize here because the success of the communication event does depend on the receiver. If understanding is to occur, the success of the communication means *you, the sender, are dependent upon the receiver.* You can't go into a communication event with a "me" attitude instead of a "we" attitude and hope to succeed.

CONCENTRATING ON THE OTHER

To successfully receiver-orient a message—and to successfully receive a message—it is essential that we concentrate on the *other,* not on ourselves and not on what we think the other might be thinking of us. If two people are primarily concerned with themselves, they will talk *at* the other, and each will miss the point. If, on the other hand, either or both is concerned primarily with how he is viewed by the other—"Am I impressing him?" "Does he think I'm smart?" Does he like my new suit?"—the communication will also fail because each has lost perspective.

The most productive discussion will be one in which each person concentrates on the other. Thus each will send messages that the other can understand: Both messages will be receiver-oriented.

The following suggestions will help to establish and maintain your concentration on the other and receiver-orient your messages.

As the sender, be attentive to the receiver by constantly soliciting feedback, and paying complete attention to that feedback. Don't wait impatiently until the receiver finishes so that you can continue with your speech. (How often do we pretend to be listening when we're really thinking, "I wish he'd hurry up and finish so I can get to my next point."?) If you begin to become too concerned with the receiver's view of you, deal with it immediately in order to reestablish understanding. Ask the receiver directly for his opinion, or ask him what he is thinking about at the moment.

As the receiver, determine what the sender is trying to accomplish and what is at stake for him. Always offer feedback with the sender in mind. If you don't understand, ask, "Would you mind going over that point again? I think you lost me." Or, "I'm not too clear on that. Does it mean this or this?" The sender may not realize that the message could be interpreted in more than one way. By giving a choice of interpretations, you tactfully point this out. Of course, it may mean neither, but the ball is then in the sender's court.

If you become entrapped in trying to make a good impression, you may be less likely to admit your confusion. But if you are receiving instructions, it is more important to understand the instructions than to leave a good impression. The impression won't last long if you fail to carry out the instructions properly. If you sense that the sender is concerned with making a good impression on you, give immediate feedback to that effect. ("You're always right on top of these things, aren't you?") Reassure him so that he can continue with his message.

Certain business situations seem to discourage keeping the receiver uppermost in your mind. For example:

Formal presentations. When you are asked to make a formal presentation, particularly to superiors, you may find yourself more concerned with the impression you're making than with whether or not they understand you. Not only may you fail to get your points across, but your anxiety can adversely affect your entire performance. (See Chapter 13.)

Sales. Often salespeople fail because they have not explained their product or service fully from the customer's (receiver's) point of view. They may become too preoccupied with making a good impression or give a spiel that they've delivered hundreds of times by rote. Instead, salespeople should put themselves in the customer's shoes. Every customer is different, so every sales talk should be too.

Being interviewed. In presenting yourself at a job interview, it is particularly difficult *not* to be aware of how others see you. However, proper preparation for the interview will allow you to receiver-orient your information *and* present yourself in the best possible light.

Giving instructions to others. It is very important to present messages containing instructions in a way that they will be understood, especially if employees will have to abide by these new instructions, policies or whatever. However, it is easy to "play boss" and lose sight of the receiver. *A word of caution:* This problem is more prevalent for managers who are not permitted to be decision-makers or to give input into decisions. If someone else makes the decisions, you might feel less need to receiver-orient these instructions. This may be more the organization's fault than it is yours. However, if *you* feel powerless, think how your subordinates must feel. Instead of "punishing" them for a situation that neither of you can help, you must manage them as you would like to be managed by giving instructions that they can understand and accept.

Performance appraisals. Performance appraisals will go much better if you base them on facts, not on opinions and general impressions of an employee's work, personality, or behavior. The key is to have documentation about a subordinate's job performance. The supervisor who doesn't really have the facts or is proceeding on "gut feel" puts the employee on the defensive. A communication breakdown can almost be guaranteed. Instead of trying to understand each other, both become defensive.

Performance appraisals don't have to be emotionally charged if the boss goes in with the facts, and if *the employee has been getting continuous feedback all along.* Then both can relax and try to view the performance from the other's perspective. Of all business situations, the performance appraisal needs to be the most receiver-oriented. The burden of proof is on the boss. He or she must present the evaluation so that the employee can understand, accept, and agree to improve.

BE EXPLICIT

Words must be handled with care. Since words have more than one meaning and since meanings frequently shift, we sometimes find that communications we thought were solidly constructed were actually built on sand.

Assuming, then, that you sincerely want to say exactly what you mean, you must choose the right words. The choice is not made any easier by the fact that there are fads and fashions in words, as in everything else. The trendy word of the moment is not necessarily the word that says what you mean. (The word *trendy,* incidentally, is an example of a trendy word.) These words come and go: in the 1960s, *charismatic* was used for every politician who could make a speech without putting an audience to sleep. The first restaurant critic who used the word *ambience* started another trend; now a restaurant review cannot be written without it. In the last decade, anything not (metaphorically at least) dead became *viable. Impact*, or a "forceful contact or collision," now is used loosely for any kind of influence or effect, or it is used as a verb. Often, in the pressure of the moment, we choose the easy word, the trendy word, whether or not it's accurate.

All words can be placed on a continuum from formal to informal, from the most denotative (exact, unemotional) to the most connotative (emotional, suggestive), and from the most general (abstract) to the most specific (detailed, precise).

Formal language often lends dignity to an occasion, but it can also be a means of "distancing" people. There are formal sentence structures as well as formal words. For example, the passive voice in conversation both dignifies and distances. "When was this done?" has a more formal, dignified and distant ring to it than, "When did you do it?" (Note that the personal pronoun is omitted; this construction is *impersonal*.) In general, the impersonality of formal words and sentences tend to chill interpersonal interchanges. Usually, informal choices are warmer and more pleasant.

In general, we choose denotative, less emotional words when we want to be accurate and objective. Connotative words, used to great effect by poets and advertisers, are more persuasive and subtly influence the receiver's attitude. Is a person aristocratic or snobbish, childlike or childish, serious or morose? It all depends upon the speaker's choice of words, which either reveal or conceal his point of view.

This is an aspect of language that could be put to work for you more than it usually is. As the initiator of a communication, the words you choose will inevitably influence the attitudes of your listeners. Why not choose to influence these attitudes in a positive way? Is the situation a "problem" or a "challenge"? The word you choose to describe it will influence how your listeners see it. *The words themselves will define the situation without any further comment from you.* Is a piece of machinery *broken* or *defective?* Is that employee *ambitious* or *power hungry?* Once you have chosen a word, it will be extremely difficult for either sender or receiver to view a situation or a person any other way during the discussion.

Tones, as well as words, can suggest various meanings. People can be amazingly insensitive to the tone of the words they choose. "Are you finished?" is a question, while "Aren't you finished yet?" is an accusation. "What's the matter?" is politely neutral, but "What's the matter with you" is hostile.

The real meaning of a word or expression resides not in the words themselves, not in the definitions in the dictionary, but in the minds of the users. "Words don't mean; people mean." The responsible communicator who wants to receiver-orient his or her message must become sensitive not only to the intended connotations of his words or tone, but also to the possibly different connotations his words might carry in the minds of his listeners.

THE ABSTRACTION LADDER

"We think in generalities; we live in detail." These words from Alfred North Whitehead aptly describe a problem with language. Words can be organized into hierarchies, from the most detailed and specific to the more general and abstract. In a sense, abstractions and generalizations ignore the qualities that things do *not* have in common. But these are necessary falsifications. Abstractions make discussion possible; we generalize in order to think.

This hierarchical arrangement of words may be a little clearer if we use linguist S. I. Hayakawa's "abstraction ladder," which looks like an ascending staircase.

At each step upward, the word becomes more general and vague. At the very bottom is the specific, an IBM Selec-

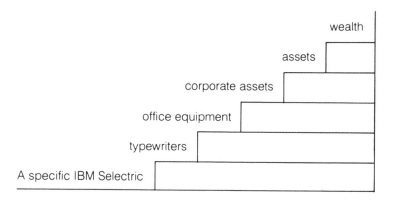

tric typewriter. It belongs to a group of machines, typewriters, which can be pictured easily. Typewriters, in turn,
belong within the class of office equipment, which may
include calculators, computer terminals, and file cabinets.
We probably have no trouble mentally picturing them. But
from office equipment to corporate assets to wealth, something happens. Corporate assets may also include lands,
buildings, and machinery, but it's a little harder to picture
because we don't know where the list ends. By the time we
get to the high level abstractions, "assets" and "wealth," so
much could be included that we could not possibly get it all
into a mental picture.

At the higher levels of abstraction, all thought of individuals disappears. When someone says "wealthy," who is
going to think of that IBM Selectric? Attempting to picture
"wealth," one person might get a mental image of a man-
sion on an estate, one might see a pile of gold bullion,
another might see oil wells, a fourth stocks and bonds, etc.

But of course, the whole point of abstractions is that you
don't need to picture them. And there is no problem as long
as you're manipulating the abstractions in your thinking.
The trouble comes when you or someone else has to translate them into detailed specifics and have the same meaning be understood by everyone.

In *The Rational Manager*, Charles Kepner and Benjamin
Tregoe outline a discussion that four managers have about
company problems. Each manager uses the word *problem*,

but each means something different by it. One manager means figures that seem out of line, while the others think in terms of inventory, customer complaints, and personnel. In the heat of the discussion, this confusion goes unnoticed because everyone uses the same word, although each has something different in mind. No solution to a problem will ever be found unless the problem is stated specifically. This means *moving down the abstraction ladder* to the lowest level on which a common definition is found that will be understood by each receiver. Many people think that they are being specific, but they are not specific enough. If the discussion has been up around the level of "assets," "office equipment" will seem specific. But if the problem is some malfunction that only typewriters are susceptible to, "office equipment" won't do it.

Your education and training have enormously increased the number of abstract words at your disposal, but they have also made word selection all that more important. If your explanations are not getting through and your discussions lead nowhere, you may be trapped at the top of the abstraction ladder. Move down step by step and be more specific. Numbers are specific, names are specific, sources of information are specific, and an exact quote is specific. Often it takes time to get to the bottom, but "getting to the bottom of it" expresses exactly where the communication will be found that gets the job done—usually at the bottom of the abstraction ladder.

GIVING INSTRUCTIONS

Giving instructions and explanations are an important part of every manager's job. Following certain principles, as described below, will make that job much easier.

We have already given the first rule of providing clear explanations: come down the abstraction ladder and be specific. Another way to be specific is to *use examples*. Examples clarify and elucidate; they are by nature specific. But there are two precautions to take when choosing your examples: they must be appropriate (that is, they must really illustrate your point and they must be something that your receiver can relate to). Use enough examples so that your receiver can draw his or her own conclusions. This is the best way to learn. For example, "participative decision management" is an abstract term. Only by describing specific organizations and how each has put "participative decision management" into practice could anyone who was not already familiar with the concept understand it. Once the examples have been absorbed, your receiver will understand the meaning of and attribute some content to the abstract phrase. It's no longer "just words."

The following is an example from a management textbook of high-level abstract language: "All positions and procedures in the model bureaucracy are governed by regulations designed to promote its objectives while preserving unity of control and direction over its efficiently divided operation." Fifteen extremely general and abstract words appear in that sentence. Unless the receiver already has had thorough experience with a bureaucracy, the sentence will have little meaning. If you explain something that abstract, *you* must provide the examples. The receiver would then say, "Aha! So that's what a 'model bureaucracy' does." Otherwise, the receiver will remain in a complete fog.

Often *diagrams, drawings, and picture language* provide a quicker method of explanation. Perhaps a diagram or chart would save time and confusion. The more senses that your receiver can bring into play, the more quickly and efficiently he will grasp your message. If your receiver can develop a mental picture of the concept, it is often more easily understood. If you compare a bureaucracy to a pyramid, for example, the receiver can visualize a shape. That helps immediately.

The basic devices for comparing the unknown (what you want to explain) with the known (what your receiver already knows) are similes, metaphors, and analogies. If your receiver knows something about football, it would be useful to compare sending a message with sending a forward pass. If, however, your receiver has no interest in sports or is a

Zulu who never heard of football, then such a metaphor is useless. You have to know your audience.

An analogy is a more extended comparison, where several parts of the unknown are similar to the known. For example, human communication and the mechanical processing of the computer are similar, so much so that communications theory has borrowed many computer terms. Both have *input* and both need feedback to function efficiently. Both are *programmed.*

Metaphors, like abstractions, are *useful* fictions. They are so persuasive, however, that we often use them as the basis of argument as though they were facts. We can argue that "the body is a machine," forgetting that most machines were originally invented by noting the mechanical principles of the human body (the ball and joint socket, for example). Then teachers explain the human body to children by analogy with machinery. Hence, children grow up believing, "the body is a machine," ignoring all differences. Use metaphors and analogies, but don't become a victim of them.

Organize your explanations. If you want to explain a process, first organize your explanation step by step. If you have a number of points, causes, or reasons to explain, note them in order of importance. If time is short, place the most important first so that it won't be overlooked if time runs out. If you're sure of having enough time, put the most important at the end and go through the least important quickly, leading up to it. If points *a* and *b* must be understood before your listener can understand point *c*, give them in that order.

A common problem in explanations is that too much is taken for granted. If you have been familiar with a process for years, you may skip over or combine some of the steps. If your receiver doesn't understand, break down the process into smaller steps. This will eliminate such problems as, "What? You don't have the tax figures? Of course they have to be figured into the costs!" Your tone implies that any idiot knows that, but your receiver doesn't because you forgot to tell him.

Always use words that you're sure your receiver under-

stands. Remember, the purpose of explaining is to have the receiver understand, not to show off your vocabulary. Again, you must know your receiver. If in doubt, ask for feedback. This should tell you whether you have used words that are misunderstood. If the word is one that your receiver must learn because it is crucial to understanding your explanation, use the word several times *in context* (if possible, in different contexts each time). This is another way of giving examples.

All of these methods of explanation are ways of saying what you mean in ways that your receiver can understand. They are also time-tested principles of teaching. When you are the sender of information and explanations you are playing an *instructive, teaching* role, a much neglected aspect of being a manager.

EXERCISES

1. The next time you must have a lengthy talk with an employee and you want his full attention, review the six steps for the SENDER. Concentrate on one or two and apply them in "setting the stage." See if the outcome is better than usual.

2. The next time you find yourself in an argument with someone, stop and ask yourself if the problem could be one of semantics. Are you using a word that has a different meaning to the other person? If your answer is yes, go down the *abstraction ladder* and reduce the word to its lowest level. Use this and see if it helps to bring about understanding and agreement. Before you use that word again, clarify its meaning with your next receiver.

3. The next opportunity you have to give instructions to someone, review the last few pages of this chapter before you speak to them. Use examples and picture words, for instance. When you finish, ask your listeners for feedback. See if these ideas helped to clarify your instructions.

4. If you have children at home, try some of these techniques in your next conversation with one of them. Use

examples and pick words that say what you really want to say and that you feel your child will understand. See if your communication improves.

5. Collect a number of small objects found around the home or office—pencils, paperclips, pocket mirror, toothbrush, rubber bands, hand stamps. Have someone describe one of the objects, without letting you see it, so that you can name it. Change roles and *you* do the describing. Now do the exercise again, only this time describe the object by using a metaphor or simile. For example, a large paperclip might be "a roadtrack made out of wire." Which was easier to guess, the literal description or the metaphor?

6. Make a study of someone you don't know very well, such as a newcomer to your organization, a client, or a potential customer. Study him and his surroundings for nonverbal clues to his personality. Write down your impressions. Then, based on your insights, initiate an informal conversation with him. Be sure to include questions that will draw him out so that you can modify your impressions if they were inaccurate. Afterwards, evaluate the conversation. How did it go? Do you feel you know him better? Do you feel any increased rapport with him? Are there any perceptible changes in his view of you? Have you changed your view of him?

7. Monitor your own sending patterns by listening to a tape recording of one of your own conversations. As you play it back, listen for your use of (a) general or abstract words, (b) heavily connotative language, and (c) repetition of pet words or phrases, or verbal tics (uh, um, and the like). What areas need improvement?

10

One-To-One Communicating: Counseling, Confrontations, and Interviews

Suitor: "I understand you perfectly well.
Young lady: "Me? Yes—I cannot speak
well enough to be unintelligible."

JANE AUSTEN, *Northanger Abbey*

PREVIEW

1. Do any of your subordinates discuss their personal lives with you? Would you like to change that?

2. Do you discuss your personal life with any of your co-workers? Are they peers, your boss, or subordinates? How do you feel about that?

3. When you are with a good friend, do you talk more about yourself than he or she does? Are there others who seem to always want to talk about themselves around you?

4. Do you do a lot of business over the telephone? Do you spend too much time on the phone? Would you like to improve your telephone behavior?

5. Are you uncomfortable when you have to give a performance appraisal? Do you know why you feel this way or what to do about it?

6. When you are interviewing someone for a job, do you get the feeling that you should be asking certain questions that you are not asking? Do you try to put this person at ease? Do you succeed?

7. If you were to lose your job tomorrow and had to look for another one, do you think you would do well in a job interview?

8. When you find yourself in a direct confrontation with someone, do you feel you handle yourself and the situation well?

"Hi! How're ya feeling?"

"Did you hear about the new dental insurance benefits?"

"Sometimes I think Jack (the general manager) never even notices what we do down here."

"If he says that one more time, so help me, I'll . . ."

"Gee, do you really feel that way, too?"

You might send any of these messages to a co-worker on a typical day. Nothing in their content distinguishes one from another, yet all five are examples of different and distinct levels of communication that can characterize a one-to-one communications event.

In this chapter, we will take a look at communicating as a *process* that is negotiated between sender and receiver and how the level of communication which is agreed upon affects the communication itself. This knowledge will then be applied in several types of one-on-one communication situations: counseling employees, performance appraisal, interviewing, and telephoning.

Before any communication event can take place, the sender must have the cooperation of the receiver. Although the sender may begin by setting certain parameters, some of these may be changed through negotiation. Some negotiable factors in a communications event are:

1. Time allotted for the event.
2. Amount of time each talks.
3. Environment for the event (where it will take place).

4. Interruptions permitted (visitors, phone calls).
5. Degree of concentration/commitment to the event.
6. Type of language to be used (formal, informal).
7. Subject matter to be discussed and how deeply you will go into it).
8. At what level you will set the discussion.

If you share a communication history with the other person, these items may be more predictable because you have negotiated them before. For example, you can probably name offhand the people who prefer short conversations and those who will spend at least thirty minutes in your office no matter what. There are people who would feel insulted if you answered the phone in their presence and others with whom you talk very freely. Although these relationships can change, they tend to be fairly constant over a period of time. But with new people, negotiations, or a feeling-out period, will go on during the first few meetings at least.

LEVELS OF COMMUNICATION

John Powell provides a useful description of communication negotiation in his book, *Why Am I Afraid to Tell You Who I Am?* People interact, Powell says, on five different levels and they move from level to level depending on their degree of interest in building a relationship with the other.

Level 5: Cliché Conversation

This is the lowest level of human interaction, characterized by meaningless statements and clichés. Powell calls it the "noncommunication of the cocktail party, the club meeting, the neighborhood laundromat." It includes brief statements such as "Hi, how are ya?" "How's the family?" "Think it will rain?" "Cold (or hot) enough for you?" "Give me a call sometime."

For example, it's 7:55 A.M., you're racing to the elevator to get to the office on time, a co-worker is waiting for the elevator, and you say, "Hi, how are ya?" You aren't interested in a reply, but it would be rude not to extend a greeting, so you chose the cliché level.

If she agrees that your communication will be a Level 5 event, she will probably respond, "I'm fine. How're you?" This is meaningless. The two of you have negotiated a cliché level conversation, and she's abiding by the rules. If she had said, "Terrible!" or even "Absolutely fantastic!" she would have invited a different response, thus negotiating for a higher level of interaction and a lengthier conversation. In our society, the use of such phrases as "Hi, how are you?" mean nothing more than, "I am greeting you in such a way as to quickly recognize your presence and move on."

No doubt you have found yourself responding to a "How are you?" with something like, "Gosh, I really feel lousy. I had something over the weekend kind of like the flu . . ." Then the listener may begin to back away a few steps, shuffle his feet, or make restless hand gestures. In this case, the listener wanted a Level 5 conversation, but you were responding on Level 4.

During a typical workday, we use many Level 5 communications simply because we would not have time, energy, or interest to use a deeper level with every person we encountered. Cliché conversation provides us with instantly acceptable words for brief communication events.

Level 4: Talking About the Weather

The next level of interaction, like the cliché level, is relatively shallow and commonplace, but it provides for a longer interaction and an increased amount of information sharing. However, the information shared is *neutral*. Neither person may be willing at this point to share important information about himself, but he is willing to extend the conversation.

Neutral topics are the weather, the news, a social event, a current business transaction, sports scores—in a word, *small talk,* which doesn't require the person to take a stand. Although Level 4 conversations are relatively brief, they can be extended for long periods if so negotiated by the participants.

To continue our Level 5 example, the co-worker with whom you exchanged greetings at the elevator is still standing there with you and you find out that something is wrong with the elevator. You will have to stand there and wait a few minutes longer. You might negotiate nonverbally to do so in silence, or you might negotiate a Level 4 conversation, such as "Did you hear about the new policy on stock options?" or "Did you see the game last night?"

None of this requires much risk on the sender's part (unless, of course, it's highly confidential information). But it does fill up the time and allows both parties to decide whether or not they want to move up to the next level together.

Level 3:   Sharing Ideas and Judgments

The elevator has just arrived, but you and your co-worker have hit upon a topic that you have mutually agreed that you would like to pursue in more depth. So you agree to continue your conversation over morning coffee in the cafeteria. By agreeing to this arrangement, you have negotiated a longer interaction and possibly a new level of communication, Level 3.

This is the first level that reveals the self and requires the persons to share their ideas and to express opinions and judgments. It involves some degree of risk because the other person may feel differently. He or she may even feel so strongly that your opinions—and even you yourself—will be rejected.

Early behavior during a Level 3 interaction is generally characterized by careful watching by each participant. "Does he really agree with me, or is he just being polite?"

The slightest raised eyebrow or breaking of eye contact may send one of the participants back into a Level 4 interchange, fearful that he or she has disclosed too much.

However, if the other person seems receptive and supportive and even shares similar views, the two may continue on this level and begin to build a relationship, a friendship based on trust. Of course, the foundation of trust is the willingness and ability to risk, so Level 3 requires some risk-taking and self-disclosure. This requires time, which must be negotiated. You will only be willing to tell the other person something if he or she is willing to tell you something in return. If you find the conversation one-sided (you are on Level 3 and he or she remains on 4), you may take steps to end the conversation or move back up to the other's level.

Rarely do two people move onto the next level (Level 2) without having had several encounters and discussions on Level 3. The next level requires even greater risk and trust, and therefore it usually takes several encounters to establish a firmly negotiated base. It may be several weeks, months, or even years before two people begin to interact on deeper levels.

Level 2: "Gut-Level" Feelings

Even though you may have shared your more important ideas and perhaps even some life history with another, you have not moved from Level 3 until you begin to share more personal and emotional aspects of your life. At the point where each person feels free to share fears, joys, and angers, the interaction moves to Level 2. To do this, you must have (either overtly or covertly) agreed to be friends and to place a high degree of trust in one another. You have probably spent a great deal of time together, testing one another's reactions, feelings, self-disclosures. If you are co-workers, your interactions may be limited to lunches and coffee breaks; if social friends, you may spend leisure time together.

The amount of time spent together is largely dependent upon availability, degree of need to share, and the number of other friends to whom you can relate on Level 2. Some people reserve this level for only one or two close friends. Others have many friends and associates with whom they interact at Level 2.

Level 1:   Peak Communication

Level 1 interactions are communication events shared by people who have deep, authentic, empathetic relationships with each other. In our society, Level 1 is largely reserved for marriages, family, and intimate friendships. Level 1 interactions are rare at work because organizations are impersonal, and time doesn't permit such familiarity. Also people tend to move around on the job, and they generally seek deeper relationships in their personal lives rather than with corporate colleagues. However, *moments* of Level 1 interaction may occur on the job when a co-worker shows empathy for another or a strong sense of understanding and caring.

The five levels of communication are both separate *plateaus* on which people converse and separate *phases* that people go through in building relationships. As phases, they are useful in explaining the process of developing close friendships. Most of us would not jump immediately into a Level 2 or Level 1 conversation with someone whom we have just met. It takes time to build trust and to gain enough knowledge about another to develop empathy. (An exception is the instant intimacy that is sometimes encountered between strangers. A person will sometimes choose a seatmate on an airplane for sharing confessions precisely because they will never see each other again and the secrets can be "unloaded" without fear of future embarrassment.)

It is possible to classify all relationships at work and at leisure according to these five levels. The following is a quick, thumb-nail sketch of the characteristics of each level for ready reference. As you read it, you might be thinking about your own relationships. At what levels are they? What are the possibilities of other levels? How many people on each level?

> *Level 5: Cliché conversation.* Shallow, simple phrases and topics. Brief. Includes greatest number of people of any level. Used heavily every day, everywhere.
>
> *Level 4: Reporting on surroundings.* Neutral topics. Interactions usually last ten to twenty minutes. Involves only half as many people as cliché level, at work and leisure.
>
> *Level 3: Sharing ideas and judgments.* Beginning of self-disclosures; involves some risk. Takes more time—fifteen minutes to an hour or more. Usually reserved for co-workers considered to be friends, social friends, and family.
>
> *Level 2: "Gut-level" feelings.* Used within atmosphere of trust and mutual respect. May be very short or lengthy. Select number of friends and family; usually used sparingly in work environment. If used, reserved for small group (two to five) of co-workers.
>
> *Level 1: Peak communication.* Highest level of meaningful relationship. Involves empathy with another. May be of long or short duration. Can sometimes be wholly conveyed nonverbally—a look, a smile, etc. Reserved for only a few people throughout lifetime— marriage partner, children, intimate friends.

APPLYING THE COMMUNICATION LEVELS AT WORK

The following principles are helpful in accurately applying the five levels of communicating at work:

Principle 1: Most employees feel most comfortable in relating to others on the upper levels (5, 4, and 3), reserving Levels 2 and 1 for outside-of-work relationships.

Principle 2: Boss/subordinate relationships are usually most effective if their interaction takes place on Levels 5, 4, and 3. But some Level 3 is necessary in order to understand each other.

Principle 3: Level 2 interaction may be necessary when an employee has strong feelings that are influencing his job performance. You may need to give him a chance to release this gut feeling before he can perform well again.

Principle 4: In performance appraisal sessions, you use data to report a subordinate's job performance. Even though this could be considered a Level 4 interaction, you must also share your judgment of the data at Level 3. If this is negative, the subordinate may give you a gut level (Level 2) defensive reaction. But you will need to maintain Level 3 or 4 in order to avoid an emotionally charged interchange.

Principle 5: When you interview a job applicant interaction, it is important to move to Level 3 as quickly as possible. Read the applicant's history and work experience (Level 4) before the interview. During the interview, you want to learn as much as possible about the applicant's ability to make decisions, use good judgment, and produce new ideas (all Level 3). If you are the interviewee, you will need to demonstrate these abilities during the interview.

Principle 6: Telephone communication is a poor type of interaction to hold on Levels 2 and 1 at work (unless it's a personal call). Strong feeling expressed over the phone can sound harsh, and emotions are much more likely to be misinterpreted in the absence of visual nonverbal clues. Business calls are usually most productive when they move swiftly from Level 5 ("Hello, Joe, how are you?") to Level 4 ("Here is the information from the report") and possibly to Level 3 ("My recommendation is . . ."). If you need to kibitz, wait for an opportunity to talk in person.

Principle 7: When counseling a problem employee, try to deal with the facts of the situation (Level 3), and encourage the employee to seek a rational solution to the problem. If the employee comes to you with a severe emotional problem, advise professional help.

The five levels, while a useful concept, do not cover every conceivable type of interaction, of course. There are many communication gray areas which are hard to place. Where, for example, would you place the lateral communications that commonly occur in all-male or all-female groups, the "kidding" that is an American male ritual or the compliment-exchanging and confidence-exchanging that is a female ritual? Is the kidding a Level 5 cliché or a Level 2 because it is often quite personal in nature? Are the compliments Level 2 when they're sincere and Level 5 when they're insincere, and how can you tell?

A worker's effectiveness on the job may be determined by how well he or she can react at the correct level. A male group may expect a woman co-worker to become "one of the guys" and participate in the typical male kidding ritual (Level 4 or 5). A woman who has never been in this situation may react with a Level 2 defensiveness, which would be a mistake.

An entirely different type of reaction is called for when the kidding is intended to demean. Two advertising account executives, one male, one female, sometimes took each other's phone calls. Whenever the male executive answered the phone, he told his co-workers, "Your boyfriend (the client) wants you." After awhile, the woman worker, controlling with some effort her gut-level reaction (a steaming Level 2 confrontation in the making), informed him calmly that this remark was very unprofessional and she would like him to stop it. (Level 4 the facts.) He did.

The games that people play in human relations outside the job are invariably games involving communication. Often, the same games are carried into the office, fouling up communications. This is especially true of rigid sex-role stereotypes. A man, for instance, may use women at work for his Level 2 confidences no matter how inappropriate they are for their work relationship. Or a woman may have no problem communicating with men when they are in traditional roles (male boss, female secretary), but she can't communicate with a male co-worker as his equal or superior.

The following story illustrates a boss/subordinate relationship that got into trouble because the level of communication went awry.

The Case of the Excellent Secretary

Barbara Hettler had been on the job for only two weeks when she was quickly promoted from a mere clerk-typist to executive secretary. John Jackson, the new vice-president sent from corporate headquarters, had been promoted over a number of more experienced candidates. It was rumored that even President Anderson had expressed some misgivings. One thing John was sure of: he had to have an efficient, loyal secretary.

Barbara's interview with Jackson had been successful. After it was over, it seemed like they had known each other for years. As soon as he hired her, he asked her opinion about how he should arrange his new office (Level 3).

Barbara remembered with pleasure that hour of moving furniture around and drawing quick floorplan sketches. Mr. Jackson seemed very attentive to every suggestion she made. Then he told her about his work patterns and what her routine would be: coffee at 7:45 A.M., mail opened and prepared for him by 9:00, coffee breaks for her roughly mid-morning and mid-afternoon, the next day's agenda to him by 4:00, etc. She was agreeable to most of it, except the 7:45 coffee. He asked her to try it for a week and then they'd sit down and talk about it. She appreciated that (Level 3).

The weeks passed swiftly. Barbara's interactions with Mr. Jackson consisted mainly of simple greetings (Level 5) and reminding him of appointments and taking dictation (Level 4). However, one day she decided to consult him about a problem (Level 2). Since she'd begun work for him, she had felt bad vibes from the president's secretary, who she felt wanted another person to have been hired for her job and now was giving her trouble. Mr. Jackson was understanding and said he'd had a similar experience, a situation that arose with another vice-president when he had first arrived (Level 2). After a lengthy conversation, Barbara left feeling good about her boss, her job, and herself.

Three months later, Barbara and John were about to go to lunch. As Barbara pondered the last few months, she thought to herself, "I probably know more about what's happening in this company than any other executive secretary." John had shared most of his experiences and insights with her and she with him. They had become a team, she thought.

John Jackson had been doing some thinking, too. He felt close to Barbara and relied heavily on her. At times it seemed she knew what he was going to say before he said it (Level 1), and she was unmistakably loyal and devoted. However, she was beginning to flaunt their relationship in front of others. She seemed to have a superior attitude, which was beginning to reflect on John. The president had even had to counsel John about it.

John wanted to alter the relationship, to move it slowly from an intimate friendship to a more professional boss/subordinate relationship (from Level 1 to Level 3.)

At lunch, the conversation began with small talk (Level 4). Barbara moved it to a discussion of the results of the budget meeting (Level 3), but John was noncomittal (Level 4). Then Barbara launched into a monologue about her decision to leave her husband of fourteen years (Level 2). John, although taken aback, listened carefully.

Then John suddenly realized that *he* had become Barbara's most intimate friend. She had learned to rely on their relationship to fill her needs and had stopped developing healthy friendships with others. She had even said, "I don't know who else to tell but you. I don't really have any other friends."

The next few weeks were rocky. John advised Barbara to seek professional help and to get advice from one of her woman friends who had faced a similar situation. He became too busy to have lunch with her and began to spend time in his office with the door closed, asking her to hold telephone calls and not disturb him. Their interactions were reduced to strictly business, and he discouraged personal conversations. He tried not to be unkind or discourteous, but slowly he changed their relationship to a more workable one (Levels 4 and 3).

Although this was difficult for Barbara, she began to develop other relationships, and she didn't leave her husband after all. Ultimately, she was able to adjust and to become even more effective at her job, separating her personal needs from her work life and again being able to offer her opinions and ideas about work to a receptive boss.

Have you ever been confronted with a similar situation? What happened? The case of Barbara Hettler illustrates the need we all have for intimate, close relationships and our need to relate on all five communication levels. John Jackson allowed his relationship with his secretary to progress up to Levels 1 and 2. When he did, he made things difficult for himself and almost destructive for her. John was fortunate to extricate himself (sometimes the only way to change such a situation is to transfer the employee). Remember Principle 2: Boss/subordinate relationships are usually most effective if they are kept on Levels 5, 4, and 3.

COUNSELING EMPLOYEES

For every boss who loves to chew people out, probably a dozen others are terrified of confrontations. Many managers make the mistake of avoiding counseling employees about problems—whether job-related or personal—because they're afraid of the conflict that could result. However, there are ways to handle the situation successfully and avoid some of the difficulties experienced by John Jackson.

If an employee comes to you with a problem that is interfering with his or her job performance, always hear the person out. Be empathetic and receptive to the employee's Level 2 messages but return Level 3 responses, such as, "I understand how you feel. Do you have any ideas how you might solve the problem?" If the problem is so severe that the employee cannot function, advise that he or she seek professional help. Never assume the role of amateur psychologist—that's not your job and it's not the best way to help your employee.

Every manager will have to become a counselor at some time or another. The following guidelines should help you communicate when that time comes.

DOs

1. Find a private place to talk.
2. Take time to listen carefully.
3. Let him talk it out.
4. Encourage him to tell you facts (not just emotions).

5. Encourage him to think of possible solutions.
6. Let him know that this is confidential.
7. Encourage him to seek other advice too (friends, family, clergyman).
8. If the problem is severe, advise professional help.
9. Encourage him to set some concrete goals for seeking a solution.
10. End the counseling session on a positive note. Confirm your belief in him.

DON'Ts

1. Don't talk in front of others.
2. Don't refuse to listen.
3. Don't interrupt him or allow yourself to be interrupted during the counseling session.
4. Don't share your own experiences.
5. Don't try to give him a solution.
6. Don't make him feel he's stupid, wrong, silly.
7. Don't encourage him to always bring his personal problems to you.
8. Don't put it on his record.
9. Don't hold it against him in the future.
10. Don't tell other employees (even your peers).
11. Don't constantly remind him of this session.

You must walk a fine line between being encouraging and empathetic but not *too* encouraging. (You don't want to become a Father/Mother Confessor in the future.) Often an empathetic ear is all that's necessary. People will frequently find their own solutions as they talk if only someone will listen.

MANAGING CONFRONTATION AND PERFORMANCE APPRAISALS

Since conflict is inevitable in human relations, every manager will encounter it at one time or another. Performance reviews, for example, can end in confrontation, whereas in some situations, the manager may deliberately invite opposition. But opposition and differences of opinion need not be unpleasant. In fact, if you know how to handle them, you can make them work for and not against you. It takes friction to get a spark that lights the fire that makes things happen. Whether the fire warms up the room or burns down the house is up to you.

In managing conflict, the most important factor is attitude, an attitude of willingness to hear others out. Given such an attitude, the following suggestions will help you to keep potentially explosive emotions under control.

1. *Be sure that the confrontation is necessary.* What will you gain from it, and will this gain be worth it in the long run? This means you must determine whether it's better to let a person air his or her feelings or to sidestep the issue.

In disagreeing with your boss, ask yourself, "Has he already decided, or can I still influence his decision?" If the decision has already been made, what new arguments can you bring up that might make him change his mind? If the answer is none, think twice about initiating the confrontation. But also decide what's at stake and what might happen if you don't speak up.

2. *Choose time and place carefully.* This is necessary in negotiating all one-to-one communication events, but it's doubly so in confrontations. If a subordinate is to be corrected, do it in private. If he's in a position to receive the message calmly, he might accept it. Nobody likes to be approached on a matter of conflict when he or she is working against a deadline, tired from a long day of meetings, or recovering from some recent defeat. Use your verbal and nonverbal listening skills to discover when the person is likely to be receptive.

3. *Try to find areas of agreement* to start from or try to discover them during the preliminary discussion. It's easier

to tolerate disagreement when some common ground, which builds rapport, has been established.

4. *Discuss the idea or the action, not the person.* It's much easier to accept criticism or disagreement when it doesn't come in the form of a personal attack. People are more likely to accept a statement that they've made a mistake, uttered in a calm tone of voice, than a charge that they're incompetent or stupid. A remark such as, "Well, you've done it again," will only put the person on the defensive.

5. *Stick to the main point.* Don't get sidetracked into minor or irrelevant issues. Stay in the present (and possible future action), not the past. This is not the time to rehearse the entire history of your relationship with this person. Unless this is a performance review, nothing is gained by rehashing past mistakes.

6. *Choose your words carefully and be diplomatic.* Say, "I believe you've made a mistake," not "You're wrong." "Please hear me out," not "When will you ever listen to me!" If the other person agrees with you, don't crow, "I told you so." He or she may regret the agreement and back off. Remember, too, that tone is as important as words. Even the most judicious words, shouted or sneered, can escalate a low-key conflict into an all-out battle.

7. *Try to create a win-win, not a win-lose, situation.* Ideally, both people in a conflict should get something out of it. If the other person concedes that you're right, you can say, "I'm so glad you agree. I think that when you see the results, you'll be pleased." (If the results are good, he may think that he thought of it himself!) If the two of you agree to continue to disagree, you can say, "Well, even if I didn't change your mind, I'm glad I had this chance to talk things over. I feel I understand your viewpoint better."

Help the other person concede by being willing to admit your own mistakes. Saying, "I'm afraid I'm partly responsible for this situation. I should have . . ." makes it easier for the other person to admit that he, too, could have been wrong. Nothing is more disarming than "I was wrong."

The person who creates ugly confrontations on the job is the person who, psychologically, *has to win* in order to bolster his ego. He will try to humiliate the other person and "rub it in" when he wins. Thus the other person can't wait to retaliate. But if you end the confrontation on a positive note, so that both of you feel that you have gained something, he'll be much more likely to be willing to listen to you next time you disagree.

8. *Try to end by agreeing on some future action.* If you are criticizing an employee, and he agrees that you are right and that there's a need to change, ask him what specifically he is going to do to make the change come about. For example, if he always fails to get reports in on time, will he rearrange his priorities, set aside more time for the reports, come in a half hour early on the day it's due? Be positive and supportive; show that you believe he's going to do it. This enables him to leave, not smarting from a scolding, but feeling that he's gained help with doing his job. The confrontation ends on a positive note. If you're disagreeing with your boss and you haven't won him over, try to get him to agree to look over your additional figures or meet at some future time to discuss it further.

9. *Above all, listen.* Make sure you understand the other person's point of view. If necessary, help him to restate his view until you do understand it. Otherwise, you'll be boxing a phantom. Listen verbally and nonverbally. Watch his face. What do you see in his eyes? What you see will help you shape what you say next. If you have come on too strong and hurt his feelings, you may have to back off and give him some reassurance. Is he puzzled? Explain your point some more.

Of course, some people simply can't handle conflict. If your boss can't, you may have to suffer in silence. If a subordinate can't, you may with patience be able to teach him or her that two people can disagree yet still remain co-workers and even friends.

THE ART OF INTERVIEWING

Interviewing is viewed by many managers as a tiresome task, if not a downright hassle. Although in larger companies, personnel officers may screen prospective employees, managers will always interview them prior to hiring or promoting them from within. This interviewing session vitally influences the future relationship between manager and employee. Principle 2 (boss-subordinate relationships work best at Levels 5, 4, and 3) also applies to interviews. As the interviewer, you set the tone and determine the level of interaction and the type of information to be elicited through the questions you ask.

The typical interview lasts about a half hour, and ten to fifteen questions may be asked. The accompanying list from the 1975 Endicott Report shows fifteen questions frequently used by recruiters and employers when interviewing college graduates. Many of the questions are designed to elicit Level 3 responses: The interviewee will give opinions and judgments (questions 2, 8, and 10), elucidate career-orientation and commitment (questions 1, 3, 4, and 5), and project self-image and self-confidence (questions 6 and 7). Thus you play the role of receiver, listening carefully not only to the information given but to how it is given. Since an interview alone is a stress situation for all but the most imperturbable people, "stress" questions or a "stress test" may not be necessary unless the job itself requires handling oneself well under extreme stress

Interviewing Hints

DOs

1. Begin with Level 5—greetings and clichés.
2. Move to Level 4 to learn more about the applicant's work history and background data.
3. Re-read the resume (if available) before the interview.
4. Develop questions (based on the resume) that allow the applicant to give more information.

FROM THE 1975 ENDICOTT REPORT

1. Why did you choose the career for which you are preparing?
2. How has your college experience prepared you for a business career?
3. What do you see yourself doing five years from now?
4. What specific goals, other than those related to your occupation, have you established for yourself for the next ten years?
5. What are the most important rewards you expect in your business career?
6. What do you consider to be your greatest strengths and weaknesses?
7. Why should I hire you over many other candidates?
8. What do you think it takes to be successful in a company like ours?
9. Do you have plans for continued study? An advanced degree?
10. What have you learned from participation in extracurricular activities?
11. Are you seeking employment in a company of a certain size? Why?
12. Do you have a geographical preference? Why?
13. Will you relocate? Does relocation bother you?
14. Are you willing to travel?
15. Why did you decide to seek a position with this company?

Excerpted from "Fifty Questions Asked by Employers During the Interview with College Seniors," compiled by Frank S. Endicott, Director of Placement at Northwestern University.

5. Develop Level 3 questions that ask the applicant for opinions and judgments. Give hypothetical situations and ask the applicant how he or she would handle them.
6. Encourage the applicant to offer ideas on how he or she would do the job.
7. Give the applicant enough time to answer your questions.
8. Try to put the applicant at ease throughout; give him or her a chance to present himself favorably.
9. Try to find positive things about the applicant; don't look for the negative.
10. End the interview on a positive note by identifying what you feel are the applicant's strong points.

DON'Ts

1. Don't break any of the EEO rules (i.e., "Do you plan to have children?")
2. Don't be discourteous or rude.
3. Don't give the impression that you're in a hurry.
4. Don't put the applicant in a situation where he or she must respond emotionally (except in questions testing stress).
5. Don't rush him or her into giving you quick answers.
6. Don't argue with anything that is said.
7. Don't put him or her on the defensive.
8. Don't decide too quickly that this person won't work; give him or her a chance.
9. Don't inverview somcone if another person is going to be offered the job; you're wasting both people's time.
10. Don't promise the applicant something you can't deliver.

THE RECEIVING END: BEING THE INTERVIEWEE

If you are being interviewed for a new job, you will be primarily the sender, giving information about yourself.

However, "information" should not be defined too narrowly. If you are interviewing for a management-level job, the types of information that the company will want will go far beyond the facts of your work experience (which the interviewer can get from a resume).

The twin bases for a good interview are "know thyself" and "be prepared." If you haven't analyzed your career goals and plans, do so before the interview. Questions 1, 3, 4, and 5 will separate the serious career-minded individual from the casual job-seeker. The interviewer will also be interested in what makes you tick—what motivates you. Be prepared for such questions as: What is more important to you—the money or the type of work? There is no *right* answer; the best answer will depend on the job. To fill sales jobs, employers look for people who are motivated by money. For an administrative job, they look for people with other motivations.

Prepare answers to such questions as: "Describe yourself." "What two or three accomplishments have given you the most satisfaction?" This doesn't mean rehearsing a set piece, but it does demand some thought and perhaps a rough outline in your mind.

Some questions, if sprung on you unprepared, may render you speechless: Why should I hire you? What qualifications do you have that make you think you will be successful in business? What are your greatest strengths and weaknesses? This is no time for false modesty, but you don't want to come across as arrogant or boastful either. One experienced college career counselor advised replying to this type of question with specifics. Instead of saying, "I have a lot of organizational ability," you might (if you were a mature woman reentering the job market) say, "I was chairman of a PTA bazaar that netted more than $2,000 for the school." Did you edit a school magazine or a club newsletter? Win athletic awards? Put yourself through school by selling a product or service? Do significant volunteer work? These are all accomplishments that you can describe to enable the interviewer to draw conclusions about your abilities.

If you are asked specifically about your weaknesses, the

same career counselor advises you to state them in a positive way. Are you stubborn? "I don't give up easily—I guess that means I'm stubborn." Are you a nitpicker? "People call me a nitpicker—I guess I'm too precise, but I do pay close attention to detail." One veteran interviewer once said that the kind of answer he likes to hear is something like, "My worst fault is that I simply can't tolerate inefficiency."

One critical area in which you should be well prepared is how your particular skills and experiences will fit this particular company and job (receiver-orienting your message, again). One young woman who had majored in English in college applied for a sales job. The interviewer was openly doubtful about her qualifications, but she convinced him that her communication skills could be applied in sales, and he hired her. (She was quite successful, too.)

Do some research on the company. Check libraries, trade associations, and even the company's public relations department. Do you know someone who works for the company? Ask questions. Then when you are asked, "Do you have any questions about our company?" you can respond intelligently.

After you are prepared, follow these guidelines for the interview itself.

DOs

1. Maintain emotional control at all times. Do not be persuaded (or provoked) into a Level 2 (gut-level) response.
2. Take time to think through your answers to questions.
3. Speak clearly and distinctly.
4. Put energy in your words; be animated and alive when you talk.
5. Pay close attention to the nonverbal reactions of the interviewer (you'll know when you've said enough).
6. Act interested in the job. Don't try to play it cool. If you want the job, say so.
7. Assume a self-confident attitude.
8. Look for positive things about the situation.

9. Ask only important questions about the company it-self and the department you'd like to be in.
10. Relax and enjoy the experience.

DON'Ts

1. Don't rush through your responses to questions.
2. Don't try to impress the interviewer with big words and elaborate language.
3. Don't try to act like the interviewer.
4. Don't discuss personal matters that do not effect your job performance.
5. Don't denigrate yourself or your abilities.
6. Don't apologize for past experiences.
7. Don't give more information than is necessary.
8. Don't ramble on about some experience.
9. Don't say that you have abilities and experiences that you do not.
10. Don't brag or appear arrogant.
11. Don't try to interview the interviewer.
12. Don't leave without giving the interviewer informa-tion about yourself that is important for the job.
13. Don't dress inappropriately.
14. Don't criticize past employers.

Recently, Business Careers, an executive recruiting firm, published a list of the seven most important reasons why applicants fail to get top-level jobs. Interestingly, six out of the seven were revealed to prospective employers in the job interview:

1. Inability to project a special competence being sought. Level 4 and 3 information, but apparently the unsuccessful applicants had not given enough thought to *relating* their abilities to the prospective employer's needs. Perhaps they hadn't informed themselves about the needs.
2. Frequent job moves without marked advancement in salary and responsibility. This information is usually found on resumes, less directly in interviews.
3. Appearing to be emotional and subjective. This would

be demonstrated by Level 2 (gut-level) responses to questions.

4. Being aggressive and verbose.
5. Lack of clarity in expressing views. Give yourself thought time.
6. Overly critical of previous employers. Prospective employers find a negative attitude unattractive, and it appears to be gossiping. Also, the criticism might have been expressed at Level 2.
7. Poorly dressed or groomed. Appearance does matter. Find out what is appropriate attire first.

Some reasons why women in particular fail in job interviews are as follows:

1. Failure to listen and to understand the problems, resulting in failure to project the ability to do the job. If you don't understand a question, ask that it be repeated or ask perceptual-check questions until you do.
2. Unclear reasons for seeking a new position and lack of career planning. Think all this through ahead of time so that you can give clear Level 3 responses based on sound judgment.
3. Lack of knowledge about the company, its product lines, and financial picture. Do your homework.
4. Tendency to denigrate oneself or one's abilities. If you don't believe in yourself, who will?
5. Tendency to overplay a feminine role (giggling, over-animated behavior, or suggestive comments) or projection of the "weak female" image.
6. Appearing nervous and generally uptight. Relax; use your sense of humor; regard the interview as a learning experience.

TELEPHONE COMMUNICATING

Several years ago, *Fortune* magazine published the results of a survey that asked fifty board chairmen, presidents, and vice-presidents of top companies to rank the ten worst time-wasters. The telephone headed the lists, leading even such notorious time-wasting pains in the neck as meetings, mail, and paperwork. Giving performance appraisals, interviewing, and counseling are occasional communication events, but the telephone is a daily, ongoing, never-ending responsibility. The telephone is, at the same time, the manager's most valued tool. These guidelines can help you to make it even more productive:

DOs

1. Is this call necessary, or has the telephone become a habit? Could you, by waiting until you had additional information, make one call instead of three or four?
2. Use the phone for business, not for social chatting. Some ordinarily frugal business people, who used to think twice before making a long distance call, seem to go bananas when the company installs a WATTS line. If you tend to talk on and on, make a list of the points you want to cover during the call and stick to them.
3. Choose the telephone when the interaction is expected to be short. If you anticipate talking for an hour (and the person is in the same building or city), perhaps you should arrange a meeting.
4. When you initiate calls, try to choose a time period when you will be uninterrupted and when you can make several calls at once.
5. Take calls only when you will have the time to concentrate. Otherwise, call back.
6. If you need to involve more than one other person, arrange a conference call instead of three or four separate calls.
7. Speak as clearly as possible, use simple language, and speak slowly with voice inflections to help your listener understand and maintain interest in your message. Your voice will have to convey part of what is usually carried by visual cues. (This may seem obvi-

ous, but haven't you sometimes observed people on the telephone gesturing with their hands and registering a variety of facial expressions as if they could be seen?)

8. Practice the good listening skills discussed in Chapter 3.
9. Be courteous. Answer the phone by the third ring, at least. If you said you'd call at 10 A.M., do it. Try to visualize the other person, and treat the caller as you would like to be treated.
10. Keep a daily log of your phone calls for a week. Include who initiated the call, the position of the person, the subject of the conversation, the relative importance on a scale of one to five, and the amount of time. At the end of the week, see how much time was spent—and wasted.

DON'Ts

1. Don't use the telephone for a vital conversation. You need the nonverbal communication of a face-to-face meeting.
2. Don't use the telephone to reprimand someone. Do it face to face.
3. Don't use the telephone to discuss any emotionally sensitive issue.
4. Don't talk on the phone when someone is sitting in your office. Ask to return the call.
5. Don't call long distance when a quick letter will suffice, unless time is very important.
6. Don't talk too fast and slur your words.
7. Don't try to be someone you're not on the phone ("the telephone personality"). You may meet that person some day.
8. Don't use telephone operators as an outlet for your frustrations.
9. Don't try to talk on the phone, read a memo, and write a letter at the same time. The listener can usually tell that you're not paying attention.

10. Don't chew gum, make funny noises, or play the radio loudly; it's very distracting.
11. Don't be rude when someone reaches you by mistake. Try to transfer the call or give the correct number.
12. Don't transfer a call just to get rid of someone. Take the time to direct him to the right person or department.
13. Don't constantly interrupt your caller or sit for long periods of silence.
14. Don't keep a person on hold for long periods. For more than one or two minutes, take the number and call back.

On the subject of hold, one of the most obnoxious practices in the business world is to have your secretary place a call for you, "Will you hold for Mr. Bigdome?" then let the other person sit on hold while you do something else. Fortunately, this is becoming less common. If a delay is unavoidable, always inform the person every 90 to 120 seconds.

If you screen calls for a superior, remember that most people won't be upset when asked to state their business but will be annoyed (justifiably, we think) if you put them through a cross-examination before putting the call through. Say, "Ms. Adelphi is tied up at the moment (at a meeting, on another line). Can I have her call you back, or can someone else help you?" If the caller asks your boss to call back, you can then check with the boss on whether he or she wants to speak to this person or have someone else handle it.

These hints could improve sales or customer service immensely if your company does a great deal of business over the phone. If you feel that telephone communication in your company is less than it should be, check with your local phone company. Most provide a service program for businesses on telephone courtesy and usage. Your employees (and customers) might benefit from it.

EXERCISES

1. Review the five levels of communication. As you go through the day, pause from time to time and try to identify the level on which you've just been communicating. Try to estimate how much of your day you spent at each level.

2. Make a list of people you communicate with on a daily basis (include co-workers, subordinates, superiors, family, friends). Next make a second column and write down your estimate of the level of communication. Now, count the number of people in each level. Most people have more people on Levels 3, 4, and 5. Usually Levels 1 and 2 are reserved for family and close friends. Is this true with you?

3. Make another list of all the people in your adult life with whom you have had a Level 1 relationship. Did you feel truly empathetic with each of them? Most people have only ten or twelve of these relationships in a lifetime. Do you have more or less? Consider why.

4. The next time you do a performance appraisal, review the section on "managing confrontation" and select one or two points to keep in mind during the appraisal. When the session is over, test yourself: How well did you do? Go back to the list and check off the ones you feel you still need to work on.

5. The next time you interview someone, review the section on interviewing and make a list of questions that you want to cover. See if your interviewing skills improve.

6. Before you go to bed next Sunday night, determine one hour of your working day that is usually the least cluttered. Commit yourself to setting that hour aside each day of the coming week to make necessary phone calls. Beginning on Monday, take the first five or ten minutes of this hour to review the telephone hints in this chapter. See if your telephone time is more productive during this test week. At the end of the week, make a list of the hints that were the most helpful. Post the list in your office, where it can serve as a reminder.

11

Blueprinting the Successful Meeting

> To get something done, a meeting should consist of no more than three people, two of whom are absent.
>
> ANON.

PREVIEW

1. Do you often leave a meeting wondering what happened?

2. Do you conduct a regularly scheduled staff meeting? Do you often scurry around at the last minute putting together an agenda?

3. Are the majority of the meetings you attend too lengthy?

4. Do you rarely receive a formal agenda for meetings you participate in?

5. Are there usually ten or more people from different departments present at the meetings you attend? Would a better meeting result if some were eliminated?

6. Do you often go to meetings wondering what your role should be?

7. Would you consider most meetings you attend to be prepared for and planned haphazardly?

If you answered yes to five or more questions, then not only are you a fairly typical American business manager, but you *need* this chapter. If you answered yes to only two or three, you are doing something right and you should read on to find out what it is. And if "when in doubt, have a meeting" sums up the prevailing philosophy in your organization, read on.

"If I didn't have to sit in those damned meetings all day, I might get some work done!" That's a common complaint of today's manager, for whom meetings rank number 3 on *Fortune's* list of the top ten time-wasters, right behind the telephone and the mail.

Ironically, some of the most competent managers are the worst meeting leaders, and many of them know it. At the same time, they realize that meetings are a necessary evil and that knowing how to lead a successful meeting is prerequisite to entering the executive suite.

Remember Hank Ward in Chapter 1 who didn't know why he was called to a top-level meeting at corporate headquarters and didn't find out until it was almost too late? True, some of the blame was his, but most must be placed on the person who called the meeting for failing in his responsibilities—one of which is to make sure that each participant understands the meeting's purpose and the part he or she will play in it.

You can learn from these and other mistakes how to run better meetings. While this chapter will concentrate on the leader's role in meetings, the role of the participant should not be underestimated. By active speaking, and even more important, by active listening as a participant, you will build the skills you'll need when its your turn to play the role of leader.

A good leader develops the same sort of "double-minded" ability to pay attention to two things at once as the good listener discussed in Chapters 4 and 5. While one part of the brain absorbs the content of the meeting, another part monitors nonverbal behavior for the signs of which role is being played by whom at any particular time and which stage or phase the group as a whole is in. Needless to say, this is much more difficult to do in a group than on a one to one basis. It takes time to learn how to do this, and if you are a participant but not yet a leader, you can begin by observing group behavior.

This chapter and Chapter 12 correspond to the twin functions of preparation and management that go into a successful meeting. In this chapter, the mechanics of setting up a meeting will be discussed, with the emphasis in Chapter 12 on the dynamics of group interaction and the interpersonal skills that are necessary to direct a meeting toward its goal. The first is much easier to put into practice because a series of logical steps can be followed. The second is harder, since there are no fixed rules. You must play it by ear from moment to moment.

WHEN TO HAVE A MEETING

If you can accomplish your purpose by a memo, a one-to-one appointment, a telephone-conference call, or a video communication, you should think twice before calling a meeting. Meetings are necessary only when the subject is one that people may have questions about that need immediate answers (a new procedure, for example), or when a problem to be solved requires a meeting of minds and a collaboration effort. Occasionally, a group should be brought together to interact or to solve problems and keep each other up to date. Sometimes a message must be relayed simultaneously to everyone. In these cases, a meeting would be appropriate because all would have a common interest and would obtain mutual benefits.

On the other hand, don't call a meeting because you want an audience, or because it's a company tradition. And schedule a meeting on short notice only in an emergency.

If you've considered all the alternatives and you've decided that you have a valid reason for a meeting, be prepared to do some advance spadework. A productive meeting requires time and effort spent in *preparation* to prevent unpleasant surprises.

MEETING PREPARATION CHECKLIST

1. Determine the purpose.
2. Set your objectives.
3. Choose and contact the participants.
4. Choose the date, time, and place.
5. Prepare an agenda.
6. Notify the participants.
7. Set the stage.

DETERMINING THE PURPOSE

You have probably attended meetings whose *real* purpose differed from their ostensible purpose. The following advice does not apply if you're playing that type of game. We're assuming that your stated purpose will be your actual one, but you might want to examine your motives to be sure. For example, when the vice-president of a large national corporation visited local branches, he liked to call all the managers together at a luncheon meeting where each would present a report. The managers groused privately at this waste of time because he could have seen each one individually. And none of the managers gained any needed information. Indeed, if they bothered to listen, they gained a great deal of information that they didn't want or need. The stated purpose of these meetings was informational, but the real purpose was obviously ceremonial: They were engaged in a ritual performance.

What do you hope your meeting will accomplish? The main purposes of most business meetings are to exchange information and to solve problems. In informative meetings, the boss calls his or her staff together to introduce a new policy or procedure, or the staff meets to share information on the status of its activities. Giving information when you need feedback from the recipients is the purpose of an informative meeting.

Problem-solving meetings require more leadership skills and have a set of rules all their own. Among them:

1. Everyone should understand the problem. The difference between the problem as stated and the problem as understood can be enormous.
2. Each participant should have information to help solve the problem. You may want to use an ad hoc committee, a temporary committee set up to solve specific, timely problems. (However, dissolve it when the task is accomplished. Some companies have whole departments that began as ad hoc committees!)
3. Use brainstorming to produce many possible solutions or novel solutions. Use logical steps if the problem is analytical. (See Kepner and Tregoe, *The Rational Manager,* in the Bibliography.)
4. See that every participant has an opportunity to contribute (Chapter 12 discusses methods of doing this).
5. After you agree on a solution, examine it for weaknesses. Know both the positive and the negative before action is taken.

SETTING YOUR OBJECTIVES

Your meeting purpose may be relatively general (to inform employees of new provisions in your company health insurance plan, for example), but your objectives must be specific. What exact outcome do you expect? If your meeting is informative, do you want each participant to understand the information, determine how to implement the policy, or simply leave with a positive attitude about the information?

For a problem-solving meeting, you may want to take intermediate steps before determining the best solution: define the problem more precisely, develop several alternative solutions, consider one possible solution thoroughly, or offer many solutions from which the boss will choose the best. Or, after a solution has been reached, the objective of the meeting may be to determine how to implement the solution or to enlist the support of participants and their commitment to make the solution work.

Whatever your objectives, clearly state how you can reasonably hope to meet them in the time allotted for the meeting. Perhaps if your objectives are to find a solution and to determine how to implement it, one meeting may not be enough.

CHOOSING THE PARTICIPANTS

Once you know the objectives of your meeting, you are ready to consider who can best help you accomplish them. If your purpose is informative, the task is relatively easy. You need those who will be directly affected *by* the information and those who *have* information. Choose a number between five and nine, if possible. Studies show that odd-numbered groups interact better than even-numbered. Groups of five are most successful in equalizing the interaction patterns. The second-best choice is seven. Beyond nine, it becomes difficult if not impossible for all to participate.

Choose people based on *what they know,* not which department they represent. (You're solving a problem, not electing a legislature.) All too often, meetings become too large because managers insist that all departments be represented, when it might be expedient to send reports to them later. And choose people who have the *authority* to make decisions. A person may be an expert but have no decision-making authority. You need the experts as well as the authority figures. Try to select compatible personalities whenever possible, and try to avoid the overbearing personality who stifles others' participation.

If minutes are needed, determine a method of keeping them and who should do it. Could this job be rotated at each meeting? Should you tape record it? (This often makes people uncomfortable.) If so, who will transcribe the tape?

Of course, for regular staff meetings you may not be free to choose participants, but logic will tell you that not everyone has to appear at every meeting. For example, your accountant isn't necessary on a personnel problem. This sounds elementary, but surprisingly, many managers often overlook the obvious.

CONTACTING THE PARTICIPANTS

Except for regular staff meetings, the leader should contact each participant individually in order to determine convenient dates and times, explain the purpose of the meeting, advise the person about the contribution he or she is expected to make, determine any special needs he or she might have (slide projector, extension cord). And try to determine the amount of time the participant will require to give his information.

At this point, you can drum up enthusiasm and anticipation. Comments such as, "Well, it's just another one of those damned supply sessions," should be avoided. Tell each person who else is participating in case he or she might want to contact them before the meeting for additional information. This advance interpersonal work will save actual meeting time.

SELECTING THE DATE AND TIME

Certain times of day seem to be better for concentrating than others. Also, no meeting should last more than an hour and a half, which is usually the longest period that people can concentrate intensely. If an hour and a half will not give you enough time to meet your objectives, schedule more than one meeting, hold morning and afternoon sessions, or give 15- to 20-minute breaks after every 90 minutes. The best times to hold a meeting are 9:30–11:00 A.M., 6:30–8:00 P.M., or 1:30–3:00 P.M. The afternoon is the third choice because most people are more alert in the morning and early evening. However, some are not awake at 8 A.M. and others are not very good after 8 P.M. Obviously, morning is the best time. Many managers call meetings at 4 P.M., thinking that things can be wrapped up by five. However, people may be tired or generally distracted by then.

For most people, the best days of the week and the best weeks in the month are those that fall in the middle. If you can choose any day of the week for your meeting, the order would be Thursday, Wednesday, Tuesday, Friday, Monday. If you have a devoted group (or a busy one), you might consider weekends. If you work in a retail business and Saturday is a regular workday, make Saturday the fifth choice and move Monday to last.

CHOOSING THE PLACE

The environment in which you hold your meeting can set a positive atmosphere and help the group interact with each other, or it can throw everything off.

For regular in-house meetings, each person will tend to sit in the same place each time and will come to think of this place as *his*. So if these meetings have been going well, there is no reason to change. But if they are not, one of the reasons could be the setting.

The major considerations in choosing a meeting place are:

1. Meeting purpose.
2. Number of participants.
3. Projected meeting time (and availability of a particular location).
4. Special equipment needs (easel, projector, screen).
5. Refreshments (coffee and doughnuts, lunch).
6. Location (easy access for all participants).
7. Seating arrangement (conference style, open circle, arena).
8. Freedom from interruptions (away from phones, secretaries).

9. Or field trip—in the thick of the action so you can see the problem you're discussing.

Room size is important because a small group rattling around in a huge room will feel unsettled and lost. Participants may sit too far apart (especially if they have never met before this meeting) and have difficulty getting informal conversations going. On the other hand, a group crowded into a room that's too small perhaps could feel hostile at the invasion of personal space.

Consider the furnishings and whether the arrangement is flexible. A long, narrow conference table will inhibit informal interaction, particularly if it's too large. An early bird could take a seat in the middle, and as the others arrive, they will interpret his placement as a signal that the seats near him are "taken." (This is the device by which strangers invisibly rope off seats near them in public places.) Eventually, clusters of people would be scattered too far away from each other to interact comfortably. So make sure the number of seats corresponds to the number of people.

Is the furniture in the room fixed and immovable? Perhaps you'll want to spend part of the meeting time looking at a slide presentation, which requires a theater-type seating arrangement, and then break up into smaller groups for discussion. If the furniture is immovable, you will be locked into one seating arrangement.

Is the room cold and sterile or warm and inviting? In a university experiment, the highest absentee rates were found in classes held in windowless, sterile cubes and in laboratory-classrooms with fixed seats. On the other hand, warm colors will wake people up, although a room with red carpeting, red flocked wallpaper, and red velvet draperies with matching chairseats will (besides making people think they've wandered into the inside of a tomato) make them jittery in a very short while.

More and more, group leaders are holding their meetings outside the work environment. They seem to feel that escaping from the office will make participants more relaxed and thus make the meetings more productive. But don't make the mistake of the executive who took his staff to a plush resort hotel and kept the participants so busy with meetings that no one could enjoy the amenities.

Seating Arrangements

One of the major considerations in choosing a place for the meeting is the seating arrangement. There are several different ways to seat people at a meeting, depending on the purpose and size of the meeting. Each arrangement will have a different effect on the dynamics of the group.

For an information meeting where everyone's attention is directed toward one person, a theater-style room will accommodate the most people in the least space. This is best for larger meetings, but it should not be used if you want to encourage discussion.

Schoolroom style is similar to theater style, but participants are seated at desks or tables arranged in rows. Fewer people can be accommodated, but this arrangement is preferable when participants will need to work with papers or take notes.

In the banquet style, participants are seated at tables arranged in a U, with the leaders sitting at a table at the open end of the U. This is good for panel discussions or when leaders need to distribute materials to the group or help them at a workshop.

In the T formation, participants sit at one long table, and panel, leaders, or speakers sit at a table placed across one end of the participants' table. Both banquet style and T style direct all the participants' attention toward the leaders or panelists. They should not be used when you want the participants to interact with each other.

Table Arrangements

Some conference rooms have little flexibility because they come equipped with a large oblong or rectangular table that monopolizes floor space. However, you can still make some adjustments in seating arrangements around that table. For example, if you want to be highly *directive*

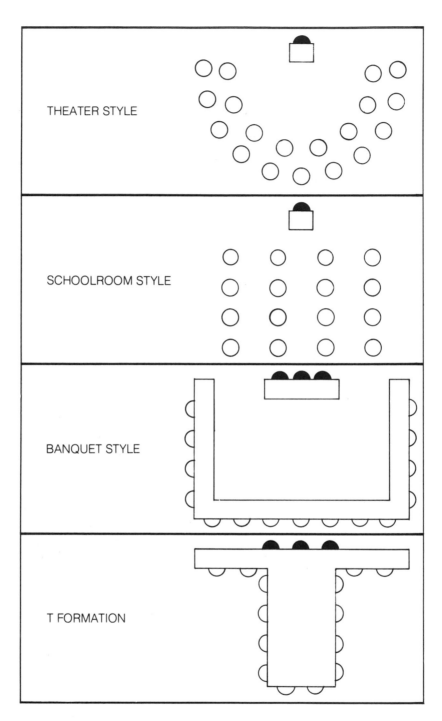

Meeting room seating arrangements.

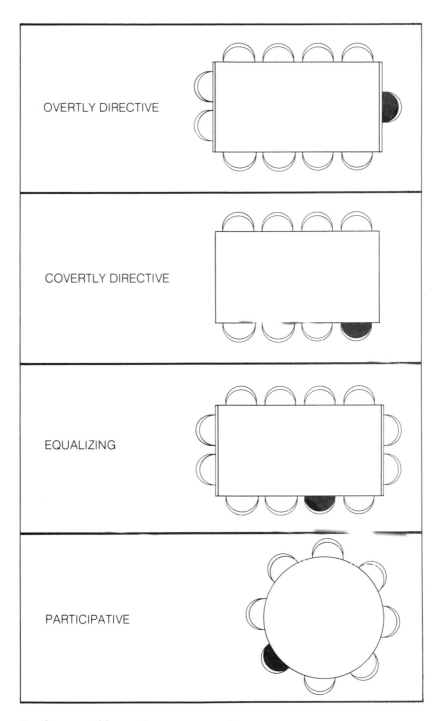

Conference table seating arrangements.

163

in your leadership style, you will want to sit at the head of the table. On the other hand, if you want to try to *equalize* the flow of communication and encourage participants to interact with each other, you will want to sit at a position that is off center or near the middle of the table.

To *look* like you are being democratic while maintaining your position of leadership (or dominance), take the end seat on one side of the table, and seat no one at the head or foot.

The most nondirective, equalizing type of seating is at a round table, and you may wish to choose a room with a round table for this reason. This would encourage greater participation and more equal sharing of information.

However, wherever the leader sits becomes the "head" of the table, and participants will still tend to direct their remarks to where they now perceive the head to be. If you are of equal or lesser status and you choose an off-center seat at a long conference table, whoever sits at the head could be perceived as the leader and could end up taking over the meeting. Whenever people meet regularly, they will arrange themselves in seats according to status, with the highest status person at the "head" and others arranged in descending order "below" the head of the table. (If you attend regular staff meetings, observe who sits where.) The seating arrangement you must *never* have is a row of chairs arranged against the outside walls of a room, which immobilizes people and prevents interchange.

If you choose the more traditional, directive arrangement, you must expect the group to look to you constantly for direction and organization. If you choose one of the more democratic and participative arrangements, you can expect more group participation. And, if you choose a highly informal, off-site location, be prepared for a certain amount of digression from the topic you came to discuss.

PREPARING AN AGENDA

An agenda must reflect as accurately as possible the actual flow of the meeting as you plan it. After planning what, where, when, why, and who, begin to plan an agenda that will allow the participants to know the direction before they start and to help you, as meeting leader, meet your objective.

Among your considerations will be the proper sequence of activities. What comes first? What must the participants understand before they can move on to something else? How much time should you allow for opening comments? How much time will each participant who is making a presentation need?

Two common errors are often made in agenda design. First is a tendency to ignore or minimize the need for *discussion* time. People will take the time anyway. Putting discussion time on the agenda will help your meeting to move along more smoothly because participants will be aware that there will be time to ask questions and make suggestions and won't interrupt during presentations. And *Discussion* on the agenda helps to remind them to hold their comments until you reach that part of the meeting. Discussions usually take longer than presentations because they are not preplanned.

The second common mistake is incorrect *sequencing* of events. Often a group called together to solve a problem will also have two or three smaller items to discuss. Small items that should take only a few minutes should be *left until the end*, much like the traditional "old business" at meetings. Most managers tend to put them first, thinking that they will quickly get them out of the way and get on to the important business of the meeting. Unfortunately, the group often never gets around to the major matters.

Another reason for putting the small items last is that they do not require as much concentration or mental energy as the more important items.

NOTIFYING THE PARTICIPANTS

Letters of notification should be timed to arrive about one to two weeks before the meeting. They should contain all the necessary information to inform the participants of what will happen at the meeting. It should contain:

1. Meeting day, time, and location.
2. Meeting purpose and objective(s).
3. Agenda (listing any special presentations with the presentors' names).
4. Names of participants and titles, when necessary.
5. Phone numbers of participants (in case they want to discuss anything with another participant before the meeting).
6. A brief description of the responsibility of the participant receiving the letter. (This means that you will have to write separate letters to each participant, of course.)
7. A personalized closing that encourages each participant to anticipate a successful meeting: "I'm looking forward to a successful goal-setting session for '85. I'm convinced that you have a valuable contribution to make. See you on the 19th!"

SETTING THE STAGE

At least a day before the meeting, you should be involved in final preparations. Make plans to arrive early on the day of the meeting to be sure that everything is ready. If you are the meeting leader, you should *always* be there first to greet the participants and make them comfortable as they arrive. If some of them do not know you or each other, exercise your interpersonal skills to put them at ease. Introduce them to each other and get informal conversation going.

But that's on the day of the meeting. A few things are still left for you to do (or to delegate) several days before the meeting. They might include some or all of the items on this checklist:

1. Double-check the room reservation.
2. Confirm the meal menus and any other refreshments ordered.
3. Confirm any special equipment needs (projector,

screen) and make sure the equipment is working and all parts are on hand (take-up reel for projector, chalk for blackboard).

4. Set up the seating arrangement.
5. Gather any additional items—pencils, notepads, gifts, and so forth.
6. Arrange for minutes to be taken or for a tape recorder to be available and in working order. (Tape is used increasingly to avoid delegating the somewhat unpleasant chore of note-taking. Your secretary can later transcribe and distribute the minutes to participants.)

IMPROMPTU MEETINGS

Although we are encouraging you throughout this chapter to plan your meetings well enough in advance to raise the probability of their success, occassionally everyone in business has a crisis that cannot wait. If an impromptu meeting is unavoidable, try to give your participants at least one hour's notice to clear the work presently in front of them and give them an estimate of how long the meeting will last. And be sure to tell them specifically what the purpose of the meeting is.

When you have the meeting, stick to the crisis at hand. Don't ramble off into other territory just because it's convenient: "Well, since I have you all together. . . ." They'll be much less willing to drop everything and run the next time. Also, respect their prior commitments. Most managers plan their day and can rarely afford to have it interrupted for 3 or 4 hours. An impromptu meeting should not last more than half an hour.

EXERCISE

1. Prepare thoroughly for your next meeting, using the blueprint in this chapter as your guide.

12

Managing the Meeting

Conference: a meeting held to decide when
the next meeting will take place.

ANON.

PREVIEW

1. When you ask, "Is there any discussion?" do you *want*
discussion? Do you get it?

2. What do you do with someone who tries to
monopolize or dominate a meeting?

3. Do you come away from your meeting feeling it accomplished what it was supposed to? Do others have the
same feeling? How do you know?

4. Do you sense subgroups forming in your meetings,
seemingly within minutes of its start? Why do they form?
What effect, if any, do they have on the success of your
meeting?

5. Can you predict how certain people will behave at
your meetings? If you don't like their behavior, can you do
something to change it?

6. Does everyone participate openly in your meetings?
If not, what can you do about it?

7. Do some people behave differently in meetings than
they do otherwise? Do they seem to play roles that are
unlike them?

8. When an argument starts in a meeting, does it usually end with one person's view prevailing? Does it end inconclusively? Do you direct the conflict productively?

You have set the stage, and the participants have arrived. Now the real work begins. Here are two examples of the possible directions your meeting might take:

Example A: *The Executive Staff*

LEADER: We look forward to having an extremely productive planning meeting today. A great deal of thought has been put into the preparation of the meeting and the agenda, and I know I'll have your full cooperation in seeing that it's carried out smoothly. As you can see, we have a great deal of business before us, so let's get started immediately on the first item on the agenda. The first item is a presentation on our financial outlook by Harry Blalock. Mr. Blalock?

BLALOCK: Thank you, Mr. Chairman. Ladies and gentlemen, I am about to distribute some figures that will show us . . ."
(Blalock speaks for about ten minutes. The other participants listen politely. A few are doodling and yawning. When discussion time is reached, they look at each other hesitantly as if to ask, "Who will be first to break the silence?" Nobody does.)

LEADER (unnerved by the awkward pause): That was very interesting. I've often thought . . . (you continue with an observation of your own for three or four minutes, then ask Blalock a question. Blalock talks for another five minutes. You, the leader, feel that probably he should be asked more questions, since he is being vague, but no one seems to have any. If you let Blalock talk much longer, you'll never get through the agenda.)

LEADER: Thank you very much, Mr. Blalock. That was very interesting. Next on the agenda is . . .

Example B: *The Gong Show*

The meeting begins late because everyone has been chatting informally. Finally, you, the leader, stand up and clear your throat.

LEADER: Well, I'm sure it's been very enjoyable to get together like this, but I guess we'd better get on with it. (The conversations die down, but you still hear a buzz from several participants. You decide to go on anyway.)

JOE WHITEMAN (interrupting): Can I say something before we actually get started?

LEADER: Sure, Joe, go ahead.

JOE: Well, Bill, maybe I shouldn't even mention this, but I notice that down here on the agenda you have an item called "new products." Now it was my understanding that the last time we had a meeting like this, we agreed that "new products" would be discussed once a year by the steering committee, and I couldn't help wondering why it was here.

LEADER: That's an interesting question, Joe, and maybe I ought to explain that . . .

IRENE (interrupting): Really, Joe, you need to be more flexible. We can't bind ourselves to every little rule when we have something new that's very hot that we need to act on immediately. Let me tell you what I think . . .

MIKE: Hey, wait a minute, folks. That item is number 8 on the agenda. What about my presentation?

JOE: We'll get to that in just a minute. But first . . .
(Whatever happened to the meeting you planned? It seems to be running away from you in every direction—and at lightning speed. If you bang the gong, you may be able to get Joe and Irene offstage and let Mike perform, but after this start, it's going to be rough to proceed in an orderly fashion through your carefully planned agenda.)

These two scenarios illustrate the two chief dangers you need to avoid in running a good meeting. When a meeting is either overdirected (Example A) or underdirected (Example B), you're in trouble.

The first example resembles meetings between the President and his Cabinet. These are strictly ritual: The real business of government is conducted elsewhere. In this example, the leader's language was formal (Mr. Blalock, not Joe), and most likely his body language was too. By emphasizing the agenda and asking for cooperation implies that he wants the participants to keep quiet and stick to his schedule. No wonder there's no discussion. Who will be the first to interfere with the smooth cogs of the machinery and cause the meeting to run overtime? When the call for discussion brings no response, the leader has no skills at his command for getting it started. So instead, he panics and talks to fill the silence. Unless the real purpose of this meeting is ceremonial, it will be unproductive: no ideas or feedback will be offered.

Scenario B will be unproductive for different reasons. It began informally, which is fine, but the leader failed to signal (either nonverbally or verbally) the end to the chitchat. When Joe brought up item 8 on the agenda, the leader took the cue and discussed it, rather than waiting until it came up later. He allowed Irene to continue this off-the-track discussion. Mike played a helpful role in trying to get back on the track, but Joe's comment shows that he has taken over the role of leader, and the real leader will have trouble regaining control.

The danger of such weak leadership is that the group's discussion will have no direction. Instead of concentrating on the objectives, this group will be too busy bickering or trying to take over the floor.

Unless you have finely honed leadership skills and experience, precise planning will not guarantee a productive meeting. The participants may turn your carefully laid plans into a shambles.

Fortunately, how people behave in groups—*group dynamics*—has received a great deal of study, and much interesting information is available to help you understand *why people act like they do* and even to predict how people *will* act in groups.

This chapter will focus first on the participant's role (the functions of members of the group); then on the developmental stages that most groups pass through, and, finally, on some typical pitfalls that often occur.

ROLE-PLAYING IN BUSINESS GROUPS

Small task-oriented groups illustrate one aspect of role-playing. Since relations between people depend on social roles, all of us participate in *group dramas*, of which business meetings are just one type. Erving Goffman's well-known book, *The Presentation of Self in Everyday Life* which first appeared in 1959, explores systematically how people in society become *performers*. When relating to others and especially to a group, we engage in the fine art of *impression management*. A person is able to function in a role before a group if he can succeed in giving the group the impression (through speech, manner, clothing, nonverbal behavior) that he is who he seems to be. How the group perceives him is important to the success of his communication with them. People will be influenced by their impression of you before you get a chance to say a word.

Everyone plays roles. Societies could not function unless individuals have clearly assigned roles and are willing to play. Roles are usually selected, not invented. Vocational choices are an example of selected roles. However, sometimes a role is *conferred*, as when an individual is promoted to a higher position. The role of "meeting leader" may be conferred upon you by your boss. You will be given no script to follow. Your success will largely depend on your understanding of the requirements of the role and your observation of how others who are successful play the role. These "others" become role models.

Role models are usually older or higher-status players, and they suggest cues to the appropriate costume, props, and actions. As you consider your role of meeting leader, you will want to observe others in your organization who play a similar role. What types of behavior do they use? Will you be able to—or even want to—imitate their style?

For example, in the discussion of seating arrangements for your meeting, did you lean toward the more "directive" or the more "democratic" arrangement. Your choice will indicate the style you choose as the meeting leader. If you feel more comfortable with the democratic arrangement, but if older executives in your organization lean toward the directive style, you may have a problem finding role models. Also as managers begin to use more democratic and participative styles of management, it is logical for the meeting-leader role to change from highly structured, controlled, and basically autocratic to one that places more emphasis on the balanced interaction and participation of all group members. But even though managers feel they should change, they may find it difficult to learn a new leadership style. Old patterns have become habits.

All roles are stereotyped to a certain extent. The audience must be able to identify the roles being played quickly and easily. Since there is little time to question each person individually as to which role he or she is playing, society prescribes forms of dress, speech, and behavior for each role. The audience thus has stereotyped expectations for the playing of each role. If someone turns out to be not what the audience expected (e.g., a man wearing an expensive business suit who turns out to be a day laborer), an audience may feel indignation because this person is masquerading as someone he's not. They feel cheated of their expectations.

Since there's no escaping audience expectations, you must decide what type of meeting-leader role you intend to play, and then play it consistently. If you want to change from an authoritarian to a more democratic style of leadership, don't jump into it too quickly. Practice first with other individuals and with smaller groups before you attempt to use it at an important meeting.

Remember that your subordinates will inevitably transfer the role you play every day as manager into the role they expect when you play meeting leader. If you make a radical change, it might frustrate and confuse them.

One autocratic manager we know tried to become more democratic and participative at his staff meetings. The first attempt totally flopped because his subordinates spent the entire meeting time trying to figure out what was wrong with him. Why wasn't he behaving normally (for him)? Why wasn't he telling them what to do? Why did he suddenly ask for their opinions? Was it some kind of a trick? He'd never done anything like this before. This manager's style had become predictable. Since his autocratic style was so well established, it was very difficult for him to change it because his audience expected it of him.

Just as participants have certain role expectations of the leader, you as leader can also expect them to play certain well-defined roles, or what sociologists define as "group-member functions." These roles are roughly either task-oriented or people-oriented. Participants playing task-oriented roles generally keep the meeting moving, stick with the agenda, try to get the job done. To them, the task at hand is more important than the people.

Participants who play people-oriented roles are more concerned with the social/political aspects of the meeting and less concerned with the accomplishment of the task. In trying to foster human interaction, they try to establish a congenial atmosphere, to be sure that everyone participates, to prevent conflict—unless it has political ramifications they're interested in.

While the two categories are not mutually exclusive, people in business meetings do tend to play one way or the other, consistent with their choice of management behavior during the workday.

Task-oriented roles can be categorized as follows:

Initiator: Gets the discussion started; starts a new topic and moves the meeting along to complete the agenda; offers direction that will help to fulfill the task at hand. (Mike in Example B.)

Informer: Gives information necessary to task fulfillment; offers ideas, teaches others, gives presentations.

Clarifier: Attempts to make a point clear; repeats another's statement to aid the group in understanding; defines and redefines the objectives or purpose of the meeting or any portion of the agenda.

Summarizer: Puts together comments in an effort to bring a topic under discussion to closure; tries to sum up in order to move on toward fulfilling the goal.

Norm-setter: Attempts to establish norms (rules) by which the group will function so as to provide structure for the meeting, i.e., coffee breaks, sticking to the agenda, setting adjournment, date for next meeting.

People-oriented roles can be defined as:

Harmonizer: Attempts to set a comfortable atmosphere; socializes, jokes, tries to make people feel at home.

Gate Keeper: Keeps lines of communication open, makes sure everyone has a chance to speak, draws out reticent people.

Consensus-seeker: Attempts to reach consensus on items requiring a decision; blocks domination and attempts to satisfy all participants; wants everyone to feel good about the results.

Compromiser: Expresses willingness to give in so that others' points of view can be considered also; tries to find equitable solutions to reduce conflict.

Referee: When conflict emerges, tries to lessen hostility by finding points of commonality in arguments; may also provide comic relief and use other means of reducing tension.

All ten roles perform useful functions at a meeting. At times, when none of the participants will play one of the assigned roles, the leader may have to take over this function in order to keep the meeting moving smoothly. However, any one of these roles carried to extreme can become negative. Some examples of negative roles are:

Dominator: Constantly initiates and informs others of his or her point of view. Egocentric: unwilling to allow others to participate; insensitive to others' needs. (Joe in Example B.)

Blocker: Prone to argue and unwilling to see others' points of view; generally blocks the progress of the meeting by preferring conflict to compromise. (Irene in Example B.)

Out-of-field Player: Chooses inappropriate behavior for the situation; plays "clown," "child," or "playboy" at the expense of others.

Hidden-agenda supporter: Operates on the basis of a private agenda that is different from the formal one; clarifies or harmonizes in ways that will further a personal objective, i.e., making one's own department come out looking good at the expense of the rest of the company.

If you know the participants at your meeting, you can probably predict the type of role each will assume. People who meet regularly with the same group tend to play the same predictable role or roles at every meeting.

Some typical comments of different role players:

"Well, I'm really delighted that all of you could come today, and I hope we'll all be pleased with the results of this meeting. (People-oriented)

"Well, it sounds unanimous. We're going to go with Project A then." (Task-oriented)

"Just a minute. We haven't heard from Evelyn yet. What do you think, Evelyn?" (People-oriented)

"I don't really think another opinion would change anything. We've already spent too much time on this. Let's vote." (Dominator/blocker)

And so it goes. It's a rare meeting that doesn't have all these roles present. Very often, participants even switch roles within the meeting. Although this can become confusing, it can also be interesting. The leader will be very busy indeed watching for the roles to emerge, encouraging one type of role and discouraging another according to the needs of the meeting at one time or another. It will take every ounce of concentration and skill he or she can muster.

LEADERSHIP ROLES: THE SITUATIONAL LEADER

The traditional style of the business meeting leader is task-oriented: He or she performs *administrative* functions, initiating, informing, clarifying, summarizing, and setting norms. However, studies in group dynamics indicate that these alone will not produce a successful meeting. "People functions" are also important, and more and more employees prefer leadership that expresses concern for them as people. More and more the modern manager must work toward a meaningful compromise in meetings, instead of bulldozing his own views through.

Thus the effective meeting leader must listen to the point of view of others and practice the harmonizing and gate-keeping functions that encourage them to offer their views. The effective meeting leader moves among the task-oriented and people-oriented functions as the need arises and rises to the *situation* to provide situational leadership.

The most difficult job is to make the right role choice at the right time. To have full participation, the reticent must be drawn out and the eager beavers restrained. While listening to the content of the meeting communications, the leader must also monitor the group's interaction and evaluate the meeting's progress, knowing when to initiate (without blocking someone else), when to inform (without stifling another point of view), when to summarize (without ending a discussion too soon), and when to seek consensus (without stopping a healthy brainstorming session). He or she must know when to loosen up and let the group interact on its own and when to tighten the reins to maintain direction.

A highly skilled leader in action will rely heavily on nonverbal cues. The leader gives nonverbal cues that lets participants know what's expected of them and is alert to the nonverbal cues of the group members, watching eyes and faces to know who is looking for a chance to speak, who is getting hot under the collar, and how many are bored or restless because someone has talked too long. It's a big job, but attempting it will begin to build leadership skills.

TYPES OF GROUPS

Groups meet for different reasons, and as such they can be categorized by types, as once described by Dean Barnlund, a Northwestern University speech professor.

Type 1: Friendly Groups. Groups gathered to enjoy each other's company, such as a party, coffee klatch, rap session. Since the group's purpose is social, the role choices are people-oriented.

Type 2: Cathartic Groups. People gathered for the purpose of *venting emotion:* mobs, funerals, weddings. Strong emotion is the common denominator, and the act of releasing it is heightened when done in collaboration with others. It becomes ritualistic.

Type 3: Learning Groups. People gathered for the purpose of giving and/or receiving information: classroom, study group, seminar, informational meeting. Role behaviors are usually task types with high value placed on initiating, informing, and summarizing.

Type 4: Policy-Making Groups. Usually the participants have high authority and responsibility: legislative bodies, judges, juries. Although problem-solving and task roles are predominant, people roles are also necessary to their success.

Type 5: Action Groups. People gathered to implement policy set by the policy-making group: implementation team, regiment, work team, "hanging mob." Task roles are important.

GROUP PHASES

Each group type also doubles as a *phase* that the group will go through in order to carry out its objectives.

Phase 1: Friendly or social. In the early stages of a meeting, the group members need to develop a sense of feeling at ease with each other, assuming that the group does not meet regularly. The social chitchat that goes on at the beginning, while people are still arriving, may appear meaningless, but actually it is making the participants comfortable. The more quickly that trust is established, the more easily and spontaneously the participants will interact. Here, regular groups have a decided advantage, since it takes time to build trust.

The harmonizer is the important people role in this early phase. The leader may signal that the meeting is informal by taking off his coat or loosening his tie, and he will put participants at ease by his nonverbal behavior, such as smiling or establishing eye contact.

Phase 2: Cathartic. Sometimes people come to meetings feeling strongly about something that may take place. The leader must be sensitive to nonverbal cues of pent-up feelings in the room. Often, an opportunity must be provided to allow feelings to be vented. *A word of caution:* If the pent-up emotion is anger, be sure to apply some structure (e.g., "Let's set aside ten minutes to get this off your chest,"); otherwise, the meeting can become a gripe session. However, this could be productive in the long run. You be the judge.

The roles you will need to play or encourage others to play are those of norm-setter, referee, and compromiser. The advantage of well-handled cathartic phase is its loosening-up effect on participants. The release of emotion can break the ice and free them to speak more openly during the rest of the meeting.

Phase 3: Learning. Once the group is relaxed, they should be prepared psychologically to learn. Informers must present information and clarifiers must follow through. If there are conflicts, the group will need consensus-seekers, compromisers, and referees. When the time is right, the summarizer should step in

During this phase, the leader cues the group nonverbally by his attending behavior. He watches for harmony or disagreement by noting mirroring and nonmirroring postures or for disagreement expressed in "turning away" or "withdrawn" body positioning. When nonverbal signals of boredom come through, he tries to liven things up, asking questions that speed a presentation along or providing a break or change of pace.

Phase 4: Policy-making. Once the group has done the appropriate amount of research and information gathering in the learning phase and you're sure they all understand what has been presented, it's time to move it into the decision-making or policy-making phase. This is the time for a final summarizing and for consensus-seeking. Again, you must read the group's readiness from nonverbal and verbal cues.

Phase 5: Action.   Once the policy decisions are made, the group must take action. They must know how to implement the plan, whether to report to a higher authority, make a recommendation, or decide to meet further. This completes the task of this particular group.

These phases have no time limitations. One group might complete all five phases in one meeting of an hour and a half. Another might require separate meetings for each phase. Another might accomplish Phases 1 and 2 in one meeting, require six meetings for Phase 3, then accomplish Phases 4 and 5 in the final meeting. Each group is different.

Often, in project-oriented companies, each phase is identical with a particular type of group. One team might be assigned just to research (the learning phase), another to make policy, and a third to implement it. All will take place in a structured meeting, but their procedures will differ.

CONTROLLING THE GROUP

When there is a well-defined leadership role, control of the group phases is less of a problem. However, even with a strong leader, there can be struggle for control of the group as people jockey for his favor. W. R. Bion and other theorists in group dynamics identify phases in the struggle for group control:

1. *Fight.*   The group jockeys for position by infighting. Outward displays of hostility may be concealed, but the meeting may bog down in meaningless bickering. The topic of the fight is unimportant, but the battle goes on until a victor emerges and the pecking order is established.

2. *Flight.* This is the period when those who lost the battle psychologically remove themselves mentally from the playing field and generally refuse to contribute. Or they may choose to play a blocking role, which prevents the group from moving toward its goal. These individuals are usually easily identified at a meeting. They choose flight because they feel they cannot assert themselves or gain control.

3. *Subgrouping.* During the flight period, people begin to exhibit "subgrouping" behavior. This is aided by the natural tendency of all groups to break up into two-to-three-member subgroups. Those who feel some sense of control tend to sit together and carry on private conversations, both verbal and nonverbal. The same is true of those in the out-of-control group.

Even though the subgroup phase is more comfortable for participants than the first two, it is nonproductive. The group has divided into adversary teams, which are really only a more sophisticated version of the fight stage. Subgrouping behavior is frequently seen in departments that have been at war for years. When they are thrown together at a meeting to work on a project, the adversary-grouping effect is almost instantaneous.

Changes in grouping, reflecting changes in the pecking order or in the membership of the "control" and "out-of-control" subgroups, can be signaled by changes in seating positions around a table.

4. *Dependency/Interdependency.* If something is not done to correct the situation when a group reaches the pairing stage, one of two things will happen: Either the group will resolve its conflict by shoving off the entire task on one individual or department, thus becoming *dependent* on someone, or they will bury the hatchet and learn to work together, entering *interdependence.* They learn to place loyalty toward the project ahead of individual or department rivalry and to share control so that each gets a piece of the action, and they develop respect for each other.

Obviously, some groups never reach interdependency.

They remain in one of the earlier phases, or get as far as dependency and stop. When this happens, the group may reach its goal—although with less efficiency—but it has failed as a *group*. (We expect groups to be united in working toward a common purpose.) And its leader has failed to unite it to get the job done.

Inadequate leadership and certain types of leaders actually encourage the formation of these emotional phases. The type of leader who likes to have his people "perform" for him will obviously encourage jockeying for position. Leaders who permit one or two individuals to dominate will foster flight behavior. But the leader who can share control from the beginning and make each participant feel friendly and important to the success of the common task—who thinks of the group as his team and not primarily as his audience—will move the group into interdependency much sooner, perhaps almost immediately.

An interdependent group is cohesive. It becomes a unit, sharing a common goal and a stronge sense of mutual respect. Participants need strong leadership less because they have learned to share leadership. Cohesive groups are generally highly productive with positive attitudes and a balance of task- and people-role behaviors.

Here's a case study of a group as it moves through the four sequences of moods and successfully arrives at a state of mutual interdependence where group goals can be efficiently achieved:

Lee Priest knew that he had been chosen over many qualified managers in the corporation for this job. He knew that much of the reason George Shank chose him was because of the instant rapport they established when they first met last fall at the Chicago conference. However, Lee was stunned when his boss announced his new assignment—member of the newly formed Ad Hoc Task Force to develop the five-year plan for the new products division. Shank would head the group.

At their first meeting, the ten participants introduced themselves. Some were important people, particularly Andrews and Starkey. Lee began to feel like the low man on the totem pole. Shank made the opening comments, then asked the committee for ideas on how to approach the project. Lee had already decided to sit back and observe the first meeting, and now with all the brass around him, he was even more determined to keep his mouth shut.

Andrews was the first to speak up. After a ten-minute dissertation that Lee had some trouble following, which upset him some, Starkey took the floor. Then, several more spoke. But no one seemed to really be talking to anyone else, and each seemed to have a different point of view.

Finally, after two hours of rhetoric, they broke for lunch. By the time they returned, the camps had formed. Soon Lee saw that the mild difference of opinion in the morning had developed into combat with two teams emerging—Andrew's and Starkey's. Only Lee and the director from California seemed to remain neutral. Finally, at 4:30, Shank called a halt and told everyone to sleep on it.

Shank opened the Tuesday meeting by saying, "I've given your comments a great deal of thought, and I feel inclined to support John Andrews's proposal that we begin by examining the merits of the Meteor Line." (Long pause and stunned silence.) "Is there any objection to that line of attack?" (Another painful silence.) "Good. Then let's develop our plan." Starkey was conspicuously silent for the rest of the morning.

The morning ended with the formation of three subcommittees. Lee had been able to offer some substantive ideas during the morning, and he was to chair the cost-analysis subcommittee. Andrews and Starkey headed the other two. The rest of the month would be devoted to committee work, in three-man teams.

The month passed quickly for Lee. Not only was his team proposal moving smoothly, but he was obtaining some status. Both Andrews and Starkey courted him, and Lee knew that at some point he would be put in the position of taking sides.

Finally, the day to reconvene came and the committees gave their reports to Shank. Lee presented a strong, well-documented package. Andrews's report was equally substantive, but Starkey's was a definite disappointment. Even Shank expressed concern. Three days later, Starkey left the Task Force because of an "emergency situation" at the home plant.

Lee regretted the loss of Starkey, but he felt that it was best for the task force. Thereafter, everything began to click. They produced their final report in record time, and all felt that they had made a major contribution to the industry.

The experience of Lee Priest is not unusual. Many managers attend meetings daily that are emotionally charged. Because their behavior can have wide repercussions on their careers, they must know how to handle themselves within it.

The case study illustrated a classic example of the Bion "sequence of moods" theory. The first meeting was rife with "fight" behavior. Each man jockeyed for position. The two strongest contenders, Andrews and Starkey, hoped to become Shank's right-hand man. When Starkey lost, the "flight" period began. He psychologically removed himself and went "underground" to develop new power strategies. During this phase, attempts at pairing were made when both Andrews and Starkey tried to win Lee to their side. When Starkey's report fell short and he removed himself, the Task Force began to function without the internal turmoil and became an interdependent team, fulfilling their requirements in record time. Unfortunately many groups never develop to this point of being a genuinely cohesive team.

THE PITFALLS OF "GROUPTHINK"

Although a cohesive group sounds ideal for a productive meeting, this is not always the case. The balance is a difficult one, and, in time, the group may either regress to earlier stages or move in the direction of *groupthink*. Sometimes cohesive groups begin to acquire feelings of invulnerability. They have such heightened sense of their own accomplishments that they begin to lose touch with reality. They may begin to accept simple conclusions uncritically. The group becomes void of conflict. And without conflict, the group loses its self-monitoring system, its ability to consider negative as well as positive aspects of every suggestion.

Since relatively few groups reach cohesiveness or maintain it, groupthink is not a frequent situation. However, if you see it occurring in your group, there are a number of things you can do: (1) Play devil's advocate or encourage someone else to; (2) introduce new members to upset the perfect balance; (3) have members submit their ideas in writing so they won't be influenced by others' opinions; (4) divide the group in half. Have them work on a problem independently, then have each subgroup try to pick flaws in the other group's solutions.

DEFUSING CONFLICT

Since you, as leader, are more likely to be trying to discourage rather than encourage conflict, there are some techniques for doing this that you may find useful:

1. Discuss issues, not people. (Avoid personalities and arguments *ad hominum.*) Discuss the present, not what happened in the past. (Who did what to whom when—that's ancient history.)

2. Try to set up win/win situations, not win/lose situations. You can encourage this by letting everyone contribute. Solicit opinions from each person, for example, before discussing anybody's pet idea. If someone must lose, allow him or her to lose in a way that saves face. (e.g., "Yes, I can see your point of view, and in many cases, I'd agree. But I think in this case, I like Howard's idea better because . . .") Not, "That's not a good idea!"

3. If you have someone who likes to "crow" over opponents and "get in the last word," try to bang the gavel and adjourn the meeting before he gets a chance to do it.

4. If you know two participants are antagonistic toward one another, seat them next to each other. People who sit across from each other interact more at a meeting than those who sit side by side because they can see each other's faces and are more aware of nonverbal cues.

5. Use words and expressions that stimulate discussion rather than argument: "You're right," "I hadn't thought of it that way," "That's true, but have you looked at it from this point of view?"

ENCOURAGING PARTICIPATION

1. Use positive verbal and nonverbal behavior. Show warmth, courtesy, and appreciation for their contributions. Thank people for participation. Avoid negative comments.

2. Ask each participant questions, addressing him or her by name. Avoid the type of questions that put people on the spot, especially at the beginning of the meeting when you're feeling each other out. (Opinion questions are good—e.g., "What did you think of that, Evelyn?" "Will that affect your department, Harry?")

3. Avoid the temptation to talk too much. When you ask a question (or someone else does), give the person time to answer.

4. Firmly control the dominators and the blockers who stifle other participants. Interrupt, if you must, to tell them that you'll take that up later on the agenda, or that this is not relevant and you'll discuss it later, in private. If a blocker becomes troublesome, enlist the help of the group to control him. Ask the group what they think of his statement, do they agree, and so forth.

5. Interrupt the rambler, and remind him what was being discussed, before the whole group loses interest and withdraws.

6. If you sense subgroups forming, draw them back into the main discussion with questions or call on one or both of the pair for help (with a projector, refreshments, reading figures). If this doesn't work, reseat them elsewhere at the table, then try to draw them in.

Unfortunately, you can know all the rules for planning and managing meetings, but you can still be an ineffective meeting leader. The secret is a combination of natural talent and skills in verbal and nonverbal communication and practice. There is no formula for effective meeting leadership. The effective group leader develops a sensitivity to the group at any given moment. Is conflict taking place? If so, is it healthy or unhealthy? What phase is the group in now? Should it remain here longer or move on? What roles are being played at the moment? Does the situation call for different roles and if so, which?

These questions are not easy to answer. Our first exercise is designed to give you practice in answering them. (The rest of the exercises will also serve as our chapter *summary*.)

EXERCISES

1. Obtain one or more typed transcripts from meetings that you have attended or ones in which you know the participants. Read through until you're familiar with the contents. Next, mark in the margins any roles, stages, or emotional phases that you recognize. After doing this, think about the meeting's progress. Then write in the margin (in another color) the roles or phases the group's leader should have been encouraging. After you feel familiar enough with this, try to identify them at the actual meeting while it's still going on.

2. Choose at least two of the following points to do at your next meeting. Add one more each succeeding meeting until you have done them all. Keep score on yourself and keep trying to better your record. You'll be well on your way to effective leadership!

 a. Spend the early moments putting people at ease with each other and with you.

 b. State the meeting purpose very specifically, and

 c. Make every attempt to follow your agenda but don't be a slave to it. Be sensitive to both the task and people needs of the group. If some more profitable topic emerges, pursue it. If you feel emotions need to be vented, permit this.

 d. Try to stay within your time limit.

 e. Be aware of group phases and how they affect the progress of the meeting.

 f. Try to lead your group toward cohesion and build an interdependent group.

g. When conflict arises, try to make it productive. Use diplomacy, not personalities, to guide it toward problem-solving.

h. Try to find ways that each group member can contribute. (Later, analyze the transcript to find out if everybody did—and how much each contributed.)

i. Take your own ego out of it. Don't boss the meeting—lead it.

13

Making a Profitable Presentation

Speeches are like the horns of a steer: a point
here, a point there, with a lot of bull in between.

ANON.

PREVIEW

1. Were you nervous the last time you had to give a
speech? Did your palms sweat, your mouth go dry, your
hands shake? Would you like to eliminate that kind of reaction the next time?

2. Do you try to avoid having to give speeches or formal
presentations? Do you find yourself delegating this type of
thing to your subordinates?

3. The last time you made a formal presentation in a
meeting, were there people in the audience with more
status than you (your boss, a vice-president or two)? How
well did you do? Do you think you could have done better?

4. When you start to prepare a twenty-minute speech, do
you wonder where to begin, what to say? Do you know how
to clarify your objectives?

5. Have you ever made a presentation to an outside
group (Rotary, Lions, Elks, NAACP, Little League, PTA,
Civic Association)? Did you feel more comfortable doing
that than giving a presentation at work? Why?

6. When you are giving a presentation, do you feel that you make your points as strongly as you intended to?

7. Have you ever had any formal speech training? Have you considered it? Why haven't you done it?

8. If you were asked to appear on a television talk show or news broadcast, would you accept the invitation? How would you prepare?

No doubt many business managers and potential managers and executives would prefer to appear before a firing squad than before a group to give an oral presentation. That's unfortunate, for while a firing squad is usually avoidable, giving an oral presentation is not. Whether the subject matter be zero-based budgeting, a strategic five-year plan, or some special project proposal, the oral presentation is frequently the means by which it is put before the company's decision makers.

Formal presentations are becoming a way of life. Increasingly, top management must supervise departments and divisions that perform highly technical operations, the details of which they don't understand. As the work gets more complex and the number of divisions increases, understanding the details becomes impossible. Indeed, understanding the details is not necessary, but understanding enough about the operations to make sound management decisions is. That's where the formal presentation comes in. Often, the formal presentation is the quickest way to impart necessary information to the decision-makers.

The formal presentation has great potential to influence the direction of the company. It must be succinct, accurate, and dynamic. Often, your potential as an executive may be evaluated partly on the basis of your ability to give a formal presentation. In the following pages, we will develop a blueprint for putting together an outstanding formal presentation, including how to prepare subject matter, audiovisuals, and *yourself*. We will also discuss the dynamics of the presentational situation—what to look for, how to respond to an audience and how to deal with the question and answer period.

PRESENTATION PREPARATION CHECKLIST

1. Clarify your topic and your time allotment.
2. Analyze your audience.
3. Determine your objectives.
4. Select your material.
5. Organize your material.
6. Prepare audio-visual aids.
7. Control nervousness.
8. Practice.
9. Fine-tune your delivery skills.
10. Final preparations.

Assume that you must make an important presentation to top management on a pet project. You have been given a date one month from now. Where do you begin? By preparing your material. The major source of your confidence when you give this presentation will be knowing that you are well prepared, and the key to this is through mastery of your material.

Given a month to prepare, the human thing to do is to put off the inevitable to a week or less before the presentation. But by doing that, you may omit or shortcut some of the important steps below. True, the tempo of your preparation should increase as you get closer to the date, with the last few days devoted to rehearsing and polishing. But begin the preparatory spadework *immediately*.

STEP 1: CLARIFYING YOUR TOPIC AND YOUR TIME ALLOTMENT

Since the topic of presentations is often assigned by someone else, it is essential to understand exactly what you are expected to do. Ask clarifying questions such as, "Are there certain points, figures, or people, that you would like me to emphasize?" "How would you like me to introduce the topic?" "What's the most important point that you want me to make?" "Is there anything I need to know that you haven't mentioned yet?" Only when your topic is clear in your mind are you ready to proceed with preparing your material.

Most presentations to top management range from ten to thirty minutes; the average time allotted is around twenty minutes. After that, the presentor may entertain questions from the audience, the group may engage in informal discussion with each other and the presentor, or the presentor may be excused from the meeting.

Even though your central nervous system may prefer ten minutes to thirty, in reality *the shorter the time allotted, the more difficult the task.* It is much harder to be convincing in ten minutes than in thirty. With thirty minutes, you have leeway to read your audience, provide additional information, or just relax. If your presentation is important, ten minutes is cutting it close.

Contrary to popular opinion, you will have to almost double your preparation time for a short presentation. Whatever comments you make must be condensed to only the most relevant, powerful, and convincing. You will have to be *extremely selective,* and a lot of the supporting data will have to be abbreviated or eliminated. Unless you're careful, your presentation may seem choppy and even illogical. Each word will have to earn its pay. Of course, supporting data for your conclusions can be kept ready for the question period. At that time, your thorough preparation will enable you to back up and defend what you have said.

STEP 2: ANALYZING YOUR AUDIENCE

Before you open that file cabinet, before you ask your secretary to collect those figures, and certainly before you put in a requisition for slides to use for visual aids, sit down and *think* about your audience. Who are they? How can you successfully influence, impress, or convince them?

Unless you already know your audience well, you may need to gather some information about the people who will be evaluating your presentation. The following types of information may prove useful and could either make or break your presentation.

1. *Status.* Is your audience comprised of executives, managers, customers, clients, board members, peers? Do they have more status than you do? If the answer is yes, then the stakes for you are higher. (This is particularly true if these people have some degree of control over and influence on your career.)

You will want to present yourself to those of higher status in a way that is appropriate to a person on your level. We once knew a middle manager who blew a presentation to a group of his company's vice-presidents by asking them to consider his proposal at their Friday afternoon golf game. They resented his cavalier approach and felt his mention of it was presumptuous. In their minds, he had "forgotten his place." His proposal was rejected.

However, if you are of higher status than members of your audience, this presents other problems. You may be anxious because you feel that they are expecting great things from you. Whether or not this is true, you do not want to appear condescending, nor do you want to come across as arrogant and self-important. If you are overly concerned with yourself or with making a big impression on your audience, you will be less likely to succeed.

You could have an audience of people at various status levels, some higher and some lower than yourself. This will be a mixed blessing, because you will not be able to direct your presentation to any one level. But on the other hand, you'll probably be forced to deal with them as individuals. This is positive and should be one of your goals.

2. *Influence.* Your audience may be in positions to influence those who have high status. Identify the relationships among people in the group. Who has influence over whom?

3. *Demographics.* In this category are age, sex, and background. You may want to slant your comments in a

different way for a group of conservative executives than for
a citizen's group composed of a cross section of the community.

Age and sex are only a part of it. Identifying the back-
grounds can become a complex problem. What kinds of job
histories do they have? We once knew a speaker who took a
pot shot at truck drivers in his talk, only to find out later that
one audience member owned a trucking company on the
side. Religious and ethnic jokes can also backfire.

4. *Education.* An important part of audience background is its education level. Does your audience speak
your language? That is, does it share a technical education
with you and thus a common vocabulary? If so, you have it
made. If not, you will have to translate your jargon into
plain language and use examples drawn from common experience. Otherwise, the audience will not understand you
and you will fail, no matter how well you know your subject.

5. *Experience.* Education and experience are not necessarily comparable. Your audience may have a wealth of
experience in your area, so be sure to deliver your presentation at the audience's level of understanding and expertise.

Of course, people in the audience may have more experience than you do. If so, you may want to clarify the
reason why you were chosen to give this presentation. It
may be that you can look at the subject from a different
angle from theirs.

6. *Interests.* This includes both work interests and outside interests. For example, if you are presenting a new
idea to a number of different departments, do you know the
special problems and interests of those departments and
how your idea will affect each one? What reasons might
they have for being in favor of it or opposed to it? If you
can't answer these questions, you could be in real trouble.
All specialists tend to be myopic about their specialities,
but top management needs to look at the entire picture.
Talk to people in other departments and find out their problems and points of view.

Discovering the outside interests of your audience may require some digging. What are their hobbies, leisure activities, special concerns? You can establish rapport with your audience by referring to these interests. One successful speaker we know, when addressing the National Secretaries Association, took a potshot at the IBM Executive Model typewriter. With the local bankers, she referred to a controversial decision by the county commission that affected them. This kind of information about an audience can pay great dividends.

7. *Peculiarities.* Every audience is different. When you give the same presentation to more than one group, you quickly learn that what works with one group often doesn't work with another. Some remarks may be perfect for most groups, but offend another. When President Carter spoke in Mexico, he referred to "Montezuma's revenge," a well-known joke to North Americans but puzzling and insulting to Mexicans. One manager failed miserably in a presentation to managers of another department in his company because he told a slightly off-color joke to an audience that (unknown to him) was quite religious.

Of course, you will probably not be able to cover all the bases in the search for peculiarities in a particular group. It certainly doesn't hurt to ask someone who has spoken to or knows this group of people if there is anything you should avoid saying or doing. It could mean the difference between success or failure.

Few people can afford time for a thorough audience analysis. But if you have worked in your organization for a while, you probably have more resources than you think. Tap into one of those informal information networks, or stop and think about the information resources at your disposal.

STEP 3: CLARIFYING YOUR OBJECTIVES

When you have firmly grasped the nature of your topic and audience, you will then need to firm up your objectives. Ask yourself, "Exactly what do I hope to accomplish with my presentation?"

In defining your objectives, there are three areas to consider:

1. *Information.* Do I want them to know something that they don't know now? If so, your objective is to give your audience *information.*

2. *Attitude.* Do I want them to adopt a certain feeling about a project, yourself, your department, or your organization? If so, your objective is to affect the *attitude* of your audience.

3. *Action.* Do I want them to *do* something as the result of my presentation (e.g., increase the budget, extend the deadline)? If so, then your objective is to convince them that the action you propose is necessary and move them to do something about it.

So you either want them to know, to feel, or to do something, perhaps all three. And what specifically is that "something"? You'd better get it clear in your own mind or you'll never get it clear in theirs. Unless you know the result you're shooting for, your presentation will lack focus and direction. As the old saying goes, "If you don't know where you're going, you might end up somewhere else."

Once you know your objectives, *write them down* and check to see if they are (1) specific, (2) measurable, and (3) realistic. If they are specific, they will be phrased in concrete, active words. If they are not specific, come far enough down the abstraction ladder (see Chapter 7) until they are. Even if your objectives are specific, they may not be measurable. In other words, how will you know that you have achieved them? Can you ask for a vote or get immediate oral or written feedback from the audience?

The third criterion is equally important: Are these objectives realistic? Have you bit off more than you can chew? For example, can you realistically expect to accomplish a total overview of the two-year project with additional projections for the next five years in a fifteen-minute presentation? If your reply is no, now is the time to redefine your objectives, limiting them to what you can realistically hope to accomplish.

At this point, you must also draw on what you have learned about your audience. What *can* you reasonably hope to accomplish with this group of people? If they are not the decision-makers, can you realistically ask them to take action on your proposal? Would it not be better to set objectives that would give them information about your proposal, and enlist their support so that they can then, in turn, influence the real decision-makers?

STEP 4: SELECTING YOUR MATERIAL

You have (1) clarified your topic, (2) analyzed your audience, and (3) set your specific objectives. Finally, you are ready to choose your material. Now is the time to be ruthless in applying the test of *relevance* to every piece of material that you consider. Only those items that relate specifically to your topic and will help you reach your objective with that particular audience can be included. Everything else—no matter how fascinating you find it or how nice it would sound—must be ruled out.

Experienced speakers usually follow a logical process to determine what to include. Begin by brainstorming possible subtopics. Jot down ideas as they hit you. Don't interrupt the flow of ideas to criticize each one as you write it down. Now read back through the items and cross out any that are irrelevant. Read through the ones that are left. Have you forgotten anything? If so, add it to your list.

Now you are ready to think about the natural sequence and organization of the points you have written down. Look at the accompanying chart called *Methods of Organizing Material*. Each kind of material that you have will fit into one of these categories.

METHODS OF ORGANIZING MATERIAL

Your Purpose	*Method to Use*
1. To relate a story or give the history of something	Narrative order. Tell the events in the order in which they occurred.
2. To describe how to do something	Step-by-step order. Tell how the process is done, giving each step in the order in which it is performed.
3. To classify; to argue for or against something	Logical order. Arrange the points of your classification or the points of your argument in a logical, easy-to-follow sequence.
4. To predict what effect something will have	Cause and effect. First give the causes or conditions, then discuss the probable effects. (Useful in anticipating future events.)
5. To analyze what caused something	Effect to cause. First discuss the effects, then suggest possible causes. (Useful in analyzing a present problem.)
6. To compare something	Comparison and contrast. Discuss how two or more things are alike and/or different. (Useful in identifying advantages and disadvantages of something or learning about an unknown by comparing it with something that is known.)

For example, if your proposal will accomplish some important gains for the company, each gain will be one of the "points" of your argument for it. (Method #3.) The points that you are making will need to be arranged in some kind of order. If points 1 and 2 must be understood before you can discuss point 3, then logically they must come first in your presentation. Or (especially if time is short and your audience impatient) you might begin with the most important point and follow with points in descending order of importance in case any have to be omitted. Or, if you want to lead your audience up to your most important point, you could reverse that order, saving your most important point for last.

When you have decided what you're going to do, go back through your list and number your points in the order in which you think you will present them and rearrange them in sequence. You now have a *rough outline*.

Review the outline and add a check mark next to the points that will require additional material. You have now arrived at the *information-gathering* stage. It's time to enlist the aid of your secretary in pulling files that contain specific figures, quotes, flow charts, or whatever else you think you will need.

Keep in mind that ultimately you will not use all the information, but you should gather *three times* the amount of material that you will actually use. The late President Lyndon B. Johnson said, "Cut it in half, tighten it, and leave out the damn jokes!" This is not bad advice, but in order to follow it, you must start with more than you will need.

STEP 5: ORGANIZING YOUR MATERIAL

Once you have collected most of the information and material that you think you will need, you are ready to take Lyndon Johnson's advice. The way in which you organize your information will be critical to the success of your pres-

entation. Following the steps below should aid you in organizing:

1. Collect all the materials you have gathered on your
desk in front of you. Get out your rough outline and *check
off* the items that required additional information which
you now have.

2. You are now ready to revise your rough outline. Prepare a second outline based on your additional research.
You may have uncovered additional facts that will require a
slightly different emphasis and hence a different organization. On getting further information, points that seemed
important may now seem less so. Does the sequence seem
right? Ask yourself, "What needs to come next? Should this
item come before or after this statistic?"

3. Once you have completed the second outline (this is
your real working outline), you are ready to consider an
opening and a *closing* for your presentation. The following
are some hints on effective openings and closings:

Openings

The all-important beginning moments of a presentation
set the tone for the entire event. In classic public-speaking
training, students were encouraged to use the "opening
joke" technique. Unfortunately, this method became so
stereotyped that these openings themselves became a
joke—"A funny thing happened to me on the way to the
speech tonight . . . ha, ha, ha . . . and now I would like to
speak to you about capital punishment." Opening jokes
often have nothing to do with the topic of the talk itself,
and therefore they are pointless except to relax and warm
up the audience. (They actually serve more to relax the
speaker.) Waste no time getting into your subject with
pointless jokes. Every minute counts. Your opening should
accomplish all of the following:

1. Get the attention of the audience, so they are interested in two things—your topic and you.

2. Set a positive tone and establish rapport with your audience.

3. Be consistent with your topic in order to introduce it.

4. Allow you to present yourself as relaxed and in control.

Easier said than done? That is why you often spend more time trying to think of a good opening than in preparing the rest of the speech. A stereotypic salesman might get the attention of his audience with a peppy handshake, a flashy smile, and a glossy photo of his product. As a persuasive presenter, you might do it simply with an appealing presence and excellent delivery skills. But whatever you do, you must focus attention on yourself, and off the big board meeting that starts in an hour, that irate client on the telephone, or that cocktail party tonight for the Mayor. Otherwise all of your careful preparation will be wasted.

One good way to open is with an illustrative example or anecdote. It doesn't have to be funny; it *should* be about the topic. Perhaps an example of something specific that's happening in your industry will illustrate why you feel that your proposal has merit. The ideal anecdote is brief, memorable, and *to the point.*

Another way to open is to grab your audience's attention with a startling statistic ("Did you know that this company lost umpteen thousand manhours last year because of _____?") or a surprising statement ("Everybody seems to think that xyz's product lines are profitable. But my investigation shows that they're badly mistaken.") Or take a familiar saying and turn it around so that it becomes fresh and attention-getting ("If silence is golden, then the person who can lower the efficiency-killing decibel level here will make this company a mint.")

Closings

An old, three-step speech-making axiom says, "Tell 'em what you're going to tell 'em; tell 'em; then tell 'em what you've told 'em." The last, a *summary,* is one method of closing a presentation, and often it's useful for a complex subject or one with a number of interrelated items. In case anybody's mind wandered while you were pursuing one of the items, a good summary reiterates and reminds your audience of the main point you want to leave them with. The last two or three sentences will be the *first thing* that the audience will remember about your presentation. Therefore, the closing, like the opening, must be carefully designed to help you accomplish your objectives with your particular audience. Ask yourself, "What can I say at the end that will really solidify my presentation, that will really make them know, believe, and act on my comments?"

To serve its purpose well, the closing must be powerful. You can't just come to a stop: You want a climax for your presentation, not a shutdown. And whatever you do, when you finish your closing, shut up and get off the stage, or move away from where you've been standing. Don't keep talking after your closing or you'll undo everything you've done.

NOTE: If a question and answer period is to follow, you may want to save some lucid or dramatic points or data to reveal here. If you have done your homework on audience analysis and have thoroughly researched your topic, you should be able to *predict* what questions will be asked. You should certainly give some thought to anticipated questions. And, if you have collected three times the amount of material that you can use, you will have plenty of back-up information for the question period. (Some speakers have been known to plant questions in the audience. Why not? In case no one else asks, those questions will not be overlooked.)

STEP 6: PREPARING AUDIO-VISUAL AIDS

Too often, the novice begins working on a presentation by choosing visual aids: "Gee, I've got these great slides I could show!" The trouble with that approach is that you are likely to build the presentation around the slides instead of the other way around. Don't let the tail wag the dog. Only now, when you know what you are going to say, should you begin thinking about slides or other visuals to support your presentation.

You may have been jotting down notes to yourself on possible visual needs as you went along, but not until you have completely prepared your talk are you ready to decide what media aids could enhance it.

We do encourage you to use some visual support because sight is the most powerful sense—almost *six times* as powerful as the other four: sight, 75 percent; hearing, 13 percent; touch, 6 percent; smell, 3 percent; and taste 3 percent.

What your audience sees will probably also be remembered better than what it hears. Many years ago, a young trainee had to give a practice speech at a management-training class. He slouched to the front of the room, stumbled up the platform, and dropped his notes and his glasses. Just as the audience was going numb with embarrassment, he announced his topic, "How Not to Give a Speech," the beginning of which he had just demonstrated. Now, twenty or more years later, no one remembers what he said, but they still talk about what they saw.

Carefully chosen visual aids will support and enhance your message. Some of the most helpful presentation aids are described below:

Flip chart. Probably the most widely used visual aid in business presentations, a flip chart is generally easily accessible, either as a built-in feature of most conference rooms or held on a portable easel. It can be prepared ahead of time and used spontaneously during your talk. If you are far enough away from the audience, you can even pencil notes to yourself on the borders, thus seeming to work without notes. Some hints for using a flip chart successfully include:

1. No more than ten words or figures per chart.
2. No more than 6 lines of information per chart.

3. Use a blank sheet between each sheet containing information so that the bottom one won't show through and be distracting.
4. Use tabs to separate different sections and for easy access as you manipulate the chart.
5. Practice your swing. (Swinging the top sheet over the back of the tripod can be tricky if you've never done it before.)
6. Use the last chart to summarize your major points.

Remember, the further away from you, the less some of your audience is going to be able to see. Check your chart from the back of your room for readability. For large gatherings, put less on each chart and make everything on it bigger.

Chalkboards. Most conference rooms are equipped with a chalkboard, the second most common visual aid. Like the flip chart, the chalkboard can be prepared ahead of time or used spontaneously. It has the added advantage of being erasable but the disadvantage of being messy (you could wind up with chalk dust all over your new suit). You also must turn your back on your audience as you write.

Cardboard aids. Similar to the flip chart, cardboard aids may be maps, charts, pictures, or outlines—anything you can put on a piece of cardboard with a stand-up backing. They can also be displayed on a flip-chart easel, taped on a chalkboard, or attached to a felt board (plywood covered with felt).

Handouts. Often, your presentation will include graphs, pictures, or complicated statistics that you would like your listeners to be able to take with them for future reference. A prepared handout can be passed around so that your audience will not have to take notes while you talk. Text as well as pictures can be used.

Handouts should be used with caution, however. Don't give out too much information or it will go unread, or (worse yet), the audience may begin to read while you're talking and you may never regain their attention. Never hand out anything that you don't have time to go over with your audience. "Go over," however, does not mean that you read the handout to them, which is insulting as well as boring. Instead, refer to the handout from time to time, i.e., "Now in the second paragraph, as you'll notice, the statistics show that . . ."

If you want to include line drawings, cartoons, graphs, or even photographs, have your secretary type the printed material (preferably short and in outline form for easy comprehension) and paste the drawings or other visuals on the page exactly as you want them to appear on your finished handout. You now have camera-ready copy, which you can take either to your company's printing department or to a nearby quick-print shop to be duplicated. (Some shops may make color reproductions.) If you want to use attention-getting color inexpensively, you can have your handout printed on colored stock.

If you want to use larger print on your handout than you can get from a typewriter or if you are printing your own flip charts or cardboard aids, use transfer letters from art supply or office stationery shops.

Models and samples. It can be invaluable to show an audience a small scale re-creation (e.g., an architect's model of a building, piece of equipment, or hardware), provided that they can really see it. This means that the model must be placed where everybody in the audience can see it, or passed from hand to hand, or else the audience should be given time to walk up and examine it. Instead of a model, you might bring in an actual object to demonstrate; for instance, a new piece of equipment that the audience could inspect.

Slides. Over the last few years, the use of slides in formal business presentations has greatly increased. Not only do slides make your presentation more professional, they add interest and enable you to say more in fewer words. Many larger companies have sophisticated media departments that will produce them at minimal cost. You can also take your own 35 mm slides, buy ready-made slides, or have them made from any poster, picture, drawing, or graph. If your visual is black and white, you can introduce color by sandwiching a piece of colored gelatin between the slide in the slide mount.

Here are some hints on presenting slides with your presentation:

1. Avoid overkill. Too many slides can be just as boring as none at all.

2. Make each slide count. Use one for each major idea.

3. Make your slides work for you. Never tell your audience in detail what they can see for themselves. Let the picture convey the message.

4. Use color, if possible.

5. Make sure the pictures are of good quality. If the pictures are really not that good—out of focus, off-color, badly composed—should you use them at all?

6. Intersperse pictures with words. Blend the two for more impact by combining other visual aids.

7. Have the equipment set up and ready to go long before you start.

8. Test the equipment and practice using it. Upside-down slides are embarrassing, and they waste valuable time while you reposition them in the projector.

9. Don't try to ad lib during your slide presentation. Plan what you will say during the slide presentation.

10. Position yourself in front of the screen. This is your show, not the projector's.

11. Don't turn out all the lights. Try to choose a room where you and the audience can be in the light with only the screen area in the dark.

12. Make at least your opening and closing comments with the projector off and lights on, bringing your audience's attention to you at the most important moments.

13. Don't let the slides dominate your entire presentation.

Film. Film is sometimes used in a business presentation, but it should be short. When you use film, you give up your control of the situation, and it may be difficult to regain the audience's attention. If you want to use a film, make sure it meets the following criteria:

1. Is it absolutely necessary to achieve your objectives?
2. Is the film professionally done? Informative? Interesting?
3. Is it current? No mini-skirts or '63 Oldsmobiles?
4. Is it short enough to allow you more than 50 percent of the time for your own comments?
5. Will it be new to your audience? (If the majority has seen it, simply referring to it might be enough.)
6. Will anything in it be controversial or offensive to your audience?
7. Does the film make unrelated points that will detract from your objectives?
8. Will the room provide comfortable viewing for everyone?
9. Will you be able to acquire the film, set up the necessary equipment, and preview it before the presentation?
10. Will you be in violation of any copyright laws by showing the film?

Pointers on Visual Communication

How graphics look is very important. If your company has its own audiovisual department, printing facilities, or graphics designer, you may be able to receive some valuable help in designing and making your visual aids. Although the creation of many graphics is best left to artists and designers, you can produce an effective flip chart, cardboard aid, or handout by following these pointers:

1. *Readability is your primary aim.* For maximum readability, you need *few* design elements (words or pictures) per page, *big* elements and *simple* elements (no tricky drawings with details that can't be seen beyond the first row).

2. *Contrast design elements and background.* This is essential to readability at a distance. Black on white is an obvious choice. If you want to enliven your aid with color, researchers have discovered that yellow on black or white on black closely follow black letters on white ground in readability. Other acceptable choices are white on dark blue or dark green, green on white, and red on white, in that order. The poorest choices are green on red, yellow on white, and the reverse.

3. *Keep it neat and simple.* One or two colors, styles of type, or kinds of pictorial elements per page is plenty. The more diverse the elements, the more they compete with each other for your audience's attention. Each piece of your flip chart or cardboard aid should be about *one* thing only for maximum impact. A *unified* design—one in which the viewer's eye is drawn to the center of interest—can help achieve this.

4. *Balance the design.* Balance can be either *formal* or *informal.* An arrangement is formally balanced when every element on either side of an imaginary central line matches exactly. An arrangement is informally balanced when the elements on either side of the line have the same visual weight but do not match. Informal balance is more difficult to achieve. If in doubt, formal balance is always safe.

5. *Choose a lettering style that reinforces your message.* Thick, boldface type gives an impression of strength. Gothic has an old-world flavor. Script is delicate. It would look absurd, for example, to use delicate script for heavy machinery when it's more suitable for a perfume advertisement.

No matter which visual aid you choose, always remember that *you* are the most important visual aid. What you do and how you behave is more important than any object that you use in your presentation. However, the impact of visuals is tremendous and can contribute enormously if you observe the following don'ts:

1. Don't wait until the day of the presentation to check the equipment you will be using.
2. Don't use a visual you have not previewed in advance or rehearsed with.
3. Don't twirl the pointer or toss the chalk while you're talking.
4. Don't talk to the visual; talk to the audience.
5. Don't wait until it's time to give your presentation before setting up your equipment.
6. Don't ever block the visual with your body. After you've finished with it, move away from it. The audience will then look at you and away from the visual.
7. Don't apologize for a visual. If it needs an apology, don't use it.

STEP 7: CONTROLLING NERVOUSNESS

No matter how many beautiful visuals you have prepared and how many marvelous words you have written your presentation will falter if you haven't prepared yourself both mentally and physically. To begin with, that uptight feeling, the butterflies in the stomach, are normal and even *healthy*. Most professional speakers still get nervous before an important speech. The reason is simple: It's important for them to do well, and that produces tension and starts the adrenalin flowing. Nervousness should be accepted as a natural phenomenon, and you can learn to make it work for you. There are both physical and mental ways to channel this extra energy.

Physical control. Take deep breaths before and during your presentation and relax your muscles. Walk around before you enter the room, sit in a relaxed position while you wait to go on, and do some isometric exercises at the table (such as pushing against the table with your hands and releasing). You should also prepare your voice beforehand. Try to talk to someone before you stand up.

When you are about to begin, place your feet comfortably

apart to balance your weight. Then begin to build some movement into your presentation. Walk over to your visual aid or change positions behind or in front of the rostrum. (However, don't pace because that is distracting.)

Mental control.   Of all things, the most important are to be prepared and to be confident. If you have done your homework and practiced your presentation, your self-confidence should bolster you against your nervousness. Nobody else in the room has done the amount of preparation that you have. During the time that you are in front of the audience, *you* are the expert. Assume that the audience supports you. Why shouldn't they? It is a rare audience that does not want a speaker to succeed. They want to have a pleasant, positive experience as much as you do.

Never admit your nervousness to an audience, even jokingly. Interestingly enough, even an audience that knows you is rarely aware of the degree to which you are nervous. If you call attention to your nervousness, however, the audience will begin to look for observable signs of it and soon will stop listening. Then it will be difficult to recapture their attention.

The most helpful thing you can do during the presentation is to concentrate all your attention to your audience. Think about them and you will begin to forget about yourself. This will almost automatically establish rapport with the audience. If your message is *receiver-oriented,* you have already put your audience first. You know what you want to say, you believe it's important, you've worked hard at putting it into a format that your audience can understand. Now think about how much *they* are going to benefit from understanding it and you'll be too busy to worry about yourself. If you put the audience first, you must succeed!

STEP 8: PRACTICING

People who deliver a great number of formal presentations will tell you that it is very important to practice, practice, and practice some more. The more you rehearse your presentation, the more confidence you will build, and the fewer surprises you will have on stage. In addition, not only will your mind learn the content of your talk, your body will also get used to the rhythms.

Try the following system for practicing your presentation. It has worked for many people who were learning to develop their one-to-group skills; see how it works for you.

1. Speak your presentation (using your working outline) into a *tape recorder*. Then play it back and analyze it carefully. Look for logical flow, correct language and grammar, transitions, effective opening and closing. (*Note:* Don't pay much attention to how your voice sounds. Most tape recorders distort voices. In fact, pretend you are listening to someone else. It may help you be more critical.)

2. Add the visual impact of your delivery by rehearsing the entire presentation *in front of a mirror*. Do this two or three times. Take particular notice of how you *look*. What does your body do? Are you gesturing naturally? Are you using facial expression? Do you like what you see? If so, remember it. If not, change it. Now is the time.

3. After you have practiced your presentation on tape and standing up in front of a mirror, you are ready to do it in front of a live audience. Ask a friend or two to come and listen to you. Tell them you'd like to do a dry run and you want constructive criticism. We knew a man who, after blowing an important presentation, felt bewildered because his wife had said his rehearsal was such a success. Choose someone who will not only give you constructive feedback, but who will be part of your audience or who knows what the presentation is about.

4. Practice your presentation in the *actual environment* where you will give it. Also, incorporate any *visuals* that you will be using. Again, this will eliminate the surprises, such as not knowing where the electrical outlets for the projector are or finding the rostrum too high.

STEP 9: FINE-TUNING YOUR
DELIVERY SKILLS

During the practice period, you will not only be fine-tuning your presentation itself—you should be working on your delivery skills as well. When you use the tape recorder, pay attention to your wording. When you practice in front of the mirror, pay attention to your body language. When you rehearse in front of people, you should become more aware of eye contact, voice inflection, and timing. When you incorporate visual aids, practice until you handle them smoothly and efficiently.

The delivery of your presentation is equally as important as the content. Many speakers are skilled in the area of delivery, but audiences often leave wondering exactly what they said. On the other hand, some speakers are expert in their field but have great difficulty in getting it across to others. You will be more confident if you have carefully prepared your content *and* your delivery.

Wording. Spoken English is obviously different from written English. People often do not speak in complete sentences. The following has been transcribed literally from a tape recording made during an interview: "I'm from New Jersey and I find when I was up there—and my friends who are still up in the north, when they look at Florida they think of Disney World and Circus World and Sea World, but we don't have much in the way of culture—according to them."

This is grammatically incoherent in print, but it's not incoherent to the listener. Nor is this example unusual. (The speaker was a college professor, and almost everyone speaks this way informally.) We are not suggesting that you take the example above as a model for your speech. We merely use it to make the point that you cannot prepare a speech as you would prepare a written paper. For a written paper, the sentence is the unit you will be working with. But for a speech, *the unit is the phrase.* Work with phrases; they sound like natural speech.

Your language should be conversational, direct, and simple. Avoid long, involved sentences. Avoid jargon: if even one person in your audience may not understand a term, either define it or don't use it. Practice pronouncing any words you have difficulty with or, better yet, replace them.

Body movement. Stand erect at all times. Place your feet firmly on the floor about a foot apart. When you walk, stride naturally. Taking very small steps is generally a sign of nervousness.

Gesture. Try to be natural. Some people are more naturally demonstrative than others, so if you are not a person who "talks with your hands," don't try to be. Also, don't become stiff by keeping your hands in your pockets, clasped behind you, or gripping the podium, pointer, or chalk. Let your hands fall freely by your sides, or rest them casually on the rostrum.

Facial expression. Most of the audience will be looking directly at your face. Although a deadpan expression may work for playing poker, it is usually not effective when giving a presentation. Audiences prefer speakers who are animated because they are more interesting. And don't forget to smile. It's a rare audience that doesn't appreciate a friendly smile on the face of a speaker.

Eye contact. The importance of establishing firm eye contact with the audience cannot be exaggerated. Just as we assume negative things about someone who drops their eyes in conversation, the same is true of a presentor. *You must look at your audience.*

Here are a few hints concerning eye contact in presentational speaking:

1. At the beginning and end of your presentation, pause and look out at your audience for four or five seconds. This will demonstrate your command of the situation and give the audience a chance to absorb you visually before you begin to speak.
2. Do not *read* your presentation at any point. This au-

tomatically breaks eye contact with your audience. If you *have* to read something, be sure this part of your presentation comes after you've had a chance to build rapport with the audience. Reestablish eye contact with your audience frequently as you read.

3. When using visuals, do not talk to the flip chart or the slide screen. Memorize the content so that you can face the audience when explaining it.
4. Maintain eye contact with your audience throughout your presentation. (If you are concentrating on the audience, this will occur naturally.)
5. Choose three or four people from different parts of the room to concentrate on.
6. As you talk, look directly at one person from time to time. Those sitting around him or her will sense that you are communicating directly with that person and will feel that you are concerned with establishing direct communication with them all.
7. If there is a person in the audience who appears to be hostile and worse, may interrupt you, merely avoid eye contact. By looking directly at him, you will cue in that person, giving him the opportunity to speak. Just ignore him. Look at people you feel are supportive.

Voice projection.   Be sure that you always can be heard easily by everyone in the room. On the other hand, don't shout or strain. Try to vary your voice volume. Saying something *softly* can emphasize a point as well as saying it loudly.

Voice inflection.   No one wants to listen to a monotone. Vary your pitch and inflection for interest and emphasis. This will add color and energy to your voice and make people want to listen to you. Generally keep the pitch of your voice low: It's easier to hear and carries more authority.

Timing.   Like inflection and projection of the voice, the key here is variety. If you change and alter your speaking rate, the audience won't get bored. On the other hand, don't go too slowly or too fast. (Speaking too fast is a common error made by beginning speakers.) Also, learn to use the *pause* effectively. When a speaker goes silent, it is an instant attention-getter. Skillfully placed pauses also allow the audience necessary breathers and opportunities for the information you just gave them to sink in.

Avoid distracting mannerisms. Don't play with the chalk or the pointer, twirl your hair, clench your fists, wring your hands, or stomp your feet. All divert attention from what you are saying to what you are doing. Of course, the "ums," "oh's," and "you knows" in your delivery fall into the same category.

Delivery skills are best when they are *not* observed. Instead, they should enhance and reinforce your words.

STEP 10: FINAL PREPARATIONS

At this point you should be well prepared for the actual presentation, and only a few important things remain to be done.

1. Prepare a final detailed outline of your talk two or three days before the actual presentation.
2. Gather all of your materials-visuals-equipment and put them in the correct order of delivery.
3. Have everything ready to go two days before the presentation. On the day before *do nothing at all* about your presentation. This is your "blank day." Try not to even think about it. When you go to bed the night before, briefly review your notes.
4. Eat well and get a good night's sleep the day before your talk. Your body will need the additional energy. (*Note:* Seasoned speakers have learned not to eat sweets right before a talk. It blocks your enunciation.)
5. On the day of the presentation, arrive early enough to set up and *test* any equipment that you will be using.

If possible, find the time for one last run through in the room before people arrive.

6. About an hour or so before you leave for the room, go over your final outline. If it is long, condense it to just one or two notecards consisting of only key words or phrases in the order of presentation. If you have prepared properly, you should need only very brief notes. (Whatever you do, don't write your entire presentation word for word. If you do you will either have a tendency to memorize it, in which case your delivery will sound canned or, if you take it up to the rostrum with you, you will tend to *read* it, which is equally deadly.)

ESTABLISHING AUDIENCE RAPPORT

In trying to understand why some people are more successful than others at giving formal presentations, we tried to "crawl into the heads" of a few of the most successful. We learned that each speaker/presenter goes through a series of phases when standing before an audience. Knowing these stages should help you be mentally prepared.

Stage 1: The Big I. The speaker is nervous and preoccupied with himself: "How am I doing?" "What do they think of me?" "Do they like my new suit?" "Is my slip showing?" Stage 1 is almost always a part of the opening moments of a presentation. Dr. Gregory Kunesh, Professor of Speech Communication at the University of Oklahoma, labels this stage "The Big I." If it lasts more than four or five minutes, the speaker experiences an even higher degree of anxiety. If the speaker stays in the Big I stage throughout, he or she will probably not be successful because the initial nervousness and overconcern for self becomes destructive and prevents the speaker from moving into Stages 2 and 3. The sooner you can move out of this stage, the better off you will be.

Stage 2: Into the Subject. Only by getting involved in the subject matter of the presentation can the speaker forget the Big I. The speakers who seem to really believe what they are saying, who get excited about their subject, are usually the most impressive. If you have really done your homework and are convinced that what you have to say is important, you will find it easier to become involved in your subject. If you can do that, you will soon begin to forget about being nervous. (One way to reach Stage 2 quickly is to cover something that you are particularly interested in near the beginning of your talk.)

However, giving a presentation is more than just beating your own drum about a subject that interests you. If you stay in Stage 2, you run the risk of letting the content of your message run away with you. You lose control of it—and you lose your audience. It is important to move to Stage 3.

Stage 3: Into the Audience. This is the important stage, and this is where you want to go psychologically. At this stage, you genuinely begin to concentrate on your audience. You forget about the Big I, and you capture the audience because you are gearing your message to them.

When you last listened to a good speaker, did he or she seem to be giving a "canned talk," or did it seem spontaneous—designed on the spot for that particular audience? Chances are that it was not spontaneous, but that the speaker, by concentrating on the audience, was able to adapt his or her prepared remarks to the needs of that particular audience. How was this done?

The good speaker is amazingly sensitive to an audience's nonverbal cues. When an audience is small and lights are up, the speaker watches facial expressions and body posture and movement for signs of approval, interest, disapproval, boredom, and the like. But even when the audience is large or when (as in a theater) the lights are out, the good speaker, like the trained actor, receives feedback. The audience tells the speaker where he needs to quicken his pace, tighten or eliminate material that's running too long, where he needs to draw something out, and when he's losing attention. By raising or lowering his or her voice or pausing for effect, making a gesture or changing position or even abruptly switching from one subtopic to another, he can regain its attention. The speaker can ask the audience a question, introduce an amusing anecdote that he was originally planning to save for later, ask someone in the audience to come up and assist—anything to change the pace, introduce a surprise, or increase rapport. (Note that none of these things is really possible if the speaker is still in Stage 2, or if you lost your audience at the very beginning.)

During a presentation, the rapport you establish with your audience is like a tonic. You begin to make subtle adjustments in your tone, body movements, and choice of words. The self is forgotten. This can be—and often is—totally unconscious at the time you're doing it. Only later can you look back and recall what was happening and why you had forgotten your nervousness and felt good about what you were doing. The process is also cyclical—the better you feel about what you're doing, the better the audience will feel, and the more encouragement you will get.

The secret, then, if there is one to truly great professional speaking, is first, the speaker has an important message; second, the speaker really believes in the message; and third, the speaker adjusts the presentation to each particular audience.

TELEVISION AND RADIO INTERVIEWS

The interview is a special kind of communications event: You and the interviewer are striving for the effect of *heightened conversation*. The interview is not a speech, a lecture, a monologue, or (except in special adversary situations) a debate. The ideal interviewee is one who is able to take the conversational ball and run with it long enough (but not too long). The worst kind of interviewee is one who answers a question *yes* or *no*. (If an unskilled interviewer asks you questions that call for only yes or no answers, try to expand your answer by giving some reasons.)

Successful interviewing is not only possible, but it can be easy. The interviewer will, more likely than not, be a generalist, not a specialist in your field. *You* are the specialist. Since whoever is better informed and better prepared will usually dominate the interview, this gives you an immediate built-in advantage. A lazy interviewer who has not done his or her homework will allow you by default to run the interview to suit yourself. A few top pros will know more about you than you do yourself. (But let's hope you never have to appear on "60 Minutes" or "20/20!") The majority of interviewers will probably fall somewhere in between. If you are a guest on a televised news broadcast, talk show, or local special-interest program, here are a few rules to follow to help assure your success.

Dress in subtle, solid colors. Avoid bright reds, whites, or all black, and don't wear a splashy print coat, tie, or dress. Wear comfortable clothing that doesn't bind when you are sitting. Look businesslike. Nice office attire should do it. Women should wear a bit more make-up than usual, although not too much. The lights have a tendency to wash you out.

Ask the interviewer ahead of time what kinds of questions or general categories of questions he or she will be asking you. Many times television interviewers will not give you the specific questions because they want you to react spontaneously, which is more interesting for the audience. But the host may have asked you a number of questions already—some identical to those he'll ask on the air. Make a list of questions you might be asked and formulate some logical responses. Practice putting them into words. Stage a mock interview practice session. Give someone your list and ask them to interview you. Practice your responses. If thrown a hostile or argumentative question, don't lose your composure and argue. Respond calmly with your side of the question, or change the subject if you feel unprepared to debate.

Don't eat a big meal before the appointed taping, and use the restroom first, even if you don't feel the need. Also, this will give you a chance to comb your hair or straighten your tie or hose. Be prepared for the stage area to be cold. This is often a shock to first-timers. (You think that you're shaking because you're scared, but it's really because you're cold!) It has to be, because when the lights come on, the area heats up quickly. Be prepared for the glare of the lights. You should have some time to get used to the lights before the taping starts. Adjust the microphone so that it's comfortable. After that, leave it alone. Modern mikes are incredibly sensitive.

Remember that television is a "cool" medium. Never use large gestures or a big voice. Appear calm and controlled. Let your face and voice show your animation. Don't move around too much. Look at the interviewer when he or she is talking to you, as you would naturally. When replying, the pros make eye contact with the camera, appearing to look the viewers in the eye, something you might want to practice. Be sure to locate the camera in advance. Avoid looking nervously for the camera or from interviewer to camera to technicians because you don't know *where* to look. This makes you appear shifty-eyed.

Try not to be overanxious and interrupt the interviewer. Take your time and think through your answer before you say it. But be personable, conversational, and relaxed. The more natural you are, the more appealing you will be to the viewing audience.

When the interview is over, ask the studio if you can purchase a copy of the tape. (Tapes cost about $25.) It's a great item for your personal file, and you can study it to improve your performance for any future appearances.

Radio is much easier than TV because you don't have to worry about the visual impact you're making. However, you do have to be aware of what your *voice* is doing.

Don't talk too loudly or too softly. Get a comfortable distance from the mike and then forget it. Animate your voice and use low-pitched voice tones (they carry best).

Don't use big words or technical jargon. If your language is too involved, the listener will turn the dial. Try to have a relaxed conversation with the interviewer, and don't interrupt. Try to talk with the interviewer first so that you feel comfortable with him or her and in the studio environment. Just as in the television interview, relax and be yourself.

EXERCISE

This chapter *is* the exercise. Whether you are about to give a formal presentation or do a television guest spot, follow the steps we have outlined. The task will be much simpler and much more stimulating than you may have thought possible.

14

Putting It in Writing

When you've got a thing to say,
Say it! Don't take half a day. . . .
Life is short—a fleeting vapor
Don't you fill the whole blamed paper
With a tale which, at a pinch,
Could be cornered in an inch!
Boil her down until she simmers,
Polish her until she glimmers.

JOEL CHANDLER HARRIS

PREVIEW

1. When you have to write, do you find it hard to get started? Do you spend a long time just staring at the paper?

2. Are your memos always clear and to the point?

3. Have you ever heard a writer praised because his writing sounds "as if he were talking to you"? Do you know how to do that?

4. Do you use words that you know your reader can understand? How do you know?

5. Do you know *when* to write?

6. Do you know how to organize your material before you begin a long report?

7. If you're not satisfied with your first draft, how do you go about improving it?

The best writers are usually those who can be themselves

222

on paper. When we read their writing, we feel as if a real person is speaking to us. "When we come across a natural style we are astonished and delighted, for we expected to see an author and we find a man," wrote Pascal. Most managers probably feel that good writing is beyond them. But this is not so. "As a rule," say Robert Graves and Alan Hodge in *The Reader over Your Shoulder,* "the best English is written by people without literary pretensions, who have responsible executive jobs." In a word, you.

The major goal is, of course, *to be understood.* When there are no vocal or nonverbal cues to help the reader out, and when you won't be there to answer any questions, that piece of paper has to stand on its own. That's why producing understandable writing usually takes longer and is frequently agonized over more than any other communications situation except the formal presentation.

No doubt your job regularly includes writing letters and memos, many of them probably on complex subjects. Important decisions may depend on how well your readers understand what you have written. Therefore, this chapter will concentrate on making your writing understandable. (There are many books on business writing to help you with grammar, usage, avoiding the absurdities of bureaucratese, and the like.)

Many of the principles of good speaking discussed in earlier chapters are directly applicable to good writing: clarifying your objectives, analyzing your audience, organizing your material, choosing the right words to say exactly what you mean, being specific, and so on. People who are both writers and speakers agree that a written message is more difficult to receiver-orient than is a spoken one. "Out of sight, out of mind," applies to much business writing, which tends to read as if the sender of the message had no particular receiver in mind.

This chapter will take you through the writing process and show you how to revise your writing in order to achieve simplicity, clarity, and brevity. It will also show you how to use the time you spend writing more efficiently and productively.

WHY ARE YOU WRITING?

Recently, we read an eight-page memo sent by an executive of a large corporation to his middle managers. The longer we read, the more puzzled we became. What was it supposed to be about? Were the people who got this memo supposed to do anything about it, and if so, what? Why was he telling them all this?

As the memo revealed, talking to hear yourself talk is not limited to speech, and thinking out loud with pencil and paper or dictaphone can be very helpful, but only to the writer, not to the reader. Much writing is done off the top of the head, and it should never leave the sender's desk. It is rambling, wordy, and confusing because the writer has not troubled to boil it down and get to the point. What *is* your point? That's for you to decide and to tell the reader; he shouldn't have to figure it out for himself.

If you need to, write down your thoughts in a notebook. If it's something you want to communicate to others, then use your notes as the draft for your memo or letter. If you've dictated a message, it will almost invariably have the rambling characteristics of speech, so use the dictated version as the first draft. Then revise the draft and pare it down until you have a clear, concise communication before you send it to anyone else.

You don't have time, you say? If important decisions are riding on your written words, how can you *not* take the time? If time is your problem, perhaps you could cut down on the *amount* of writing you do. Before you commit words to paper, consider whether you should write it at all. As noted in Chapter 1, the delayed feedback associated with written communication is such a drawback that other considerations must outweigh it before you decide to put it in writing. What are some of these considerations?

1. *When you need a written record.*   To prevent misunderstandings, you frequently will need to put it in writing. Things you might record in writing include anything to do with money, safety, or equal opportunity, or anything of

substance you agree to do or expect someone else to do. At some time this written record may even become a court document. You'll be glad you have it, and so will your company's lawyers.

2. *When you need to inform several people at once.* If you don't need feedback on the information you're giving, a short memo or letter with multiple copies is a great timesaver.

3. *When a piece of information should be permanent and easily retrievable.* Pulling a letter out of a file is easier than retrieving information from tape.

4. *When the message is complex.* It's more difficult to absorb complicated ideas or data by ear. In written form, they can be reread and studied.

5. *When you need to clarify and organize your own thinking.* If you have to put something into a form that's understandable to others, you will end up understanding it better yourself.

WHY SHOULD IT BE READ?

You've decided that a particular communication should be written, and you know the point you want to make. But does your reader want to read it? What's in it for him?

Every piece of writing should have a point, but it should also have a "so what?"—the reader's reason for reading it. This is a principle well known to professional writers who realize that early in an article they must give their readers some reasons for reading on or risk losing them. Often, an article will have an attention-grabbing opening paragraph or two, followed by a statement that tells the reader why he should be interested in the article, what he may hope to gain by reading it. In this way, the writer helps to receiver-orient his message.

For example, if the author of that eight-page memo had included even such a simple statement of purpose as, "Before the meeting, I'd like to give you some ideas to stimulate your thinking about our company's share of the market in the eighties," the reader would have breathed a sigh of relief.

So there are three "musts" to decide before you write:

1. What is this about? (The main point.)
2. Why should my reader be interested? (The "so what.")
3. What should my reader do about this? (The goal or purpose.)

Never let a piece of writing out of your hands until these questions are answered.

THE ANTIDOTE TO ORGANIZATIONAL STYLE

Your writing may answer all three of the above questions and still not be readable. One of the worst enemies of readable writing is what a management consultant who specializes in writing problems calls "organizational style." This style, common among businesspeople, aims for dignity and importance, but it succeeds only in being pretentious and unintelligible. Its hallmarks are a vocabulary of big, abstract words, an overabundance of words, and chilly, impersonal sentences cast mainly in the passive voice.

The obvious antidote: write simply and naturally. "Writing, when properly managed, is but a different name for conversation," wrote Laurence Sterne, the 18th-century British novelist. The key words are "properly managed." Good writing is *not* speech literally transcribed. (Read some transcripts of taped meetings if you doubt this.) Good writing sounds like a good speaker would sound if he were perfectly fluent and controlled. It only *seems* effortless.

You can produce writing that will be welcomed by your reader because it sounds like *you* talking. The best way to do this is to learn to *revise* your own writing. The much admired "conversational style" is not the result of off-the-cuff rambling on paper, but of careful revision.

The rest of this chapter will show you, step by step, how to write and revise a long memo or report. This process should also be applied to shorter writing projects, such as letters and routine memos. Follow it, and your writing will really *communicate*.

PLANNING WRITING PROJECTS

A manual on business writing recommends the following division of time for a writing project:

Worrying	10%
Planning	25%
First draft	25%
Revising to final draft	35%
Proofreading	5%

This "worrying," needless to say, is not mind-numbing anxiety but the kind of worrying a dog does a bone— turning it around, examining it from all sides, chewing on it for a while.

According to this breakdown, 35 percent of your time is used up before you even begin writing your first draft. It is spent thinking about your main point, stating and restating it until it's clear, and thinking about what your reader will need to know in order to understand your point and be persuaded of its validity. How well you use this thinking and planning time very often will determine the success or failure of your project.

Note that the first three items on the list are creative activities, and the last two are critical or analytical. Many writers get into trouble at the start because they let the critical part of their brains get control before the creative part has a chance to function. They write a sentence, look at it, decide it's no good, then waste precious time fretting about a single sentence before getting on to the next. *Don't do this.* Keep your critic under wraps in the early stages of writing. Save him for later when you'll need his help badly. If you become critical too soon, the creative part of your brain may just quit on you. Even if this doesn't happen, your project will take much longer, because you'll be fighting yourself instead of getting on with it.

Allocating Your Time

One Friday afternoon, your boss asks you to write a long memo, to be sent to the executive committee, proposing a merger of the public relations and publicity departments and including some specific suggestions on how to put the two together. For years, there's been no reason for two separate departments, and only inertia and politics have prevented the company from combining them.

You realize the decision to combine the departments has probably already been made, but a justification in writing is needed before action is taken. This doesn't make it any less important to make your proposal as convincing as possible. Also, you realize that a good plan for carrying out the merger will add to the arguments in favor of it. You have a week to write the memo.

First you need a plan of action. Until you have written many reports, it's difficult to estimate the number of hours one will take. For instance, if you already have all the facts at your fingertips, the information-gathering stage can be shortened. Some projects seem to write themselves and need very little revision, while others will take many hours to revise. However, you need at least a tentative plan. In this case, you decide on this one: Over the weekend, you'll do most of your thinking and planning. Monday morning you'll gather information and do a tentative outline. Tuesday, you'll write the first draft. Wednesday, your secretary will type your first draft and you'll devote Wednesday evening and as much time as possible on Thursday to revisions. Friday, your secretary will type the final version and you'll proofread it. This is a tight schedule. (And it's not as if you have nothing else to do!)

If you have two weeks to do your report or memo, do your first draft around the middle of the first week and your revision as close to the deadline as possible (to give yourself the longest breather you can).

Collecting Your Ideas, Clarifying Your Objectives

Throughout the weekend, whenever you have an idea, jot it down. During this worrying stage, your unconscious will probably be working on the problem while you sleep, and you may wake up with ideas you'll want to note right away. What you want to do is think of everything that should be included and what the sources of this information are. Jot down the sources of information next to the information you'll need (names of people to ask, places where information is filed). While you're doing all this, a tentative outline may be forming in your mind. If it is, fine. If not, don't push it.

The initial worrying and planning stages of your writing project correspond to the early stages of an oral presentation, described in Chapter 13. Talk it over with others— your boss, and members of the departments involved—and get their ideas. Clarify your objectives, and be sure you know your audience.

Only when you have your goal, your main idea, and your "so what" for the reader are you ready to begin writing.

Gathering Information

Before Monday morning, organize your notes. Perhaps you have scraps of paper which say things such as, "Call Joe about photo lab figures" or "Look up job descriptions of publicity dept. writers." These can serve as your "action notes" for information gathering. Go through them and arrange these tasks in the order in which you will perform them on Monday morning.

Your other notes will be "idea notes," items you plan to include in your memo. They should go in a separate folder where you will place everything as it accumulates—notes, information, outline, first draft, etc.

On Monday morning, clear your desk and begin to collect information. Use your secretary as your research assistant. (Indeed, she may know more sources of information than you do.) Not all of this may be available immediately, but don't let that deter you. When you begin to write, simply allow space in the first draft for information to come.

A note of caution: Many beginning writers outline too soon. Until you have some material to organize, you have nothing to outline. A premature outline may even prevent you from thinking of a good idea because it doesn't fit easily into your preconceived notions. You can become a prisoner of your own outline. On the other hand, later in the writing process, a good outline can help you see gaps and flaws in your thinking.

Planning Your Writing

While information is still coming in, look at your statements about your goals, main point, and "so what." Now, you will use what you know about your readers to help plan and organize your writing strategy. Your main point is that the P.R. and publicity departments should be merged. Your goal is to convince management that this should be done. Your readers should want to do this if it will make the company more efficient, reduce costs, and thus make the operation more profitable. Your strategy is to demonstrate that the merger will accomplish this.

What will you need to demonstrate this? The answer to this question will give you your *tactics*. You will have to present the problems created by separate departments and show, *in detail*, how the merger will solve these problems. These tactics are a type of analysis. The chart showing methods of organization on page 198 shows that you should use a point-by-point logical organization and a step-by-step process analysis to describe a plan for implementing the merger.

Therefore, you decide that your memo will have to have two main parts. Part I will be the point-by-point presentation of the problems and their solutions; Part II will describe how the merger should be carried out step by step.

PREPARING YOUR OUTLINE

It's late Monday morning and you still don't have an outline. Although some people write first drafts without an outline and plan on organizing the material during the revision stage, an outline is usually an invaluable guide to writing your first draft. First list your idea notes, in no particular order, like this:

1. Should save money—three publicity writers and director under-employed at present.
2. No real reason to have separate publicity department. Only happened because many years ago, R&D was headed by a former newspaperman who sent out press releases on new research and new products. This grew into publicity department. Still under R&D V.P., which doesn't make sense. Later P.R. dept. was added for producing a house magazine and newsletter. Still later, a magazine for customers was added as a P.R. organ.
3. Many functions of publicity dept. could better be handled by ad agency (better facilities for photos, etc.). This would free some time.
4. Much of what is done now by publicity largely duplicates what ad agency does.
5. Budget of publicity department high because not enough work to keep three writers busy.
6. Present Head of publicity dept. will resist merger. He'll lose prestige.
7. P.R. people not knowledgeable about media. Could use input of publicity people. Convenient to have them in same office.
8. P.R. offices nicer. Publicity would gain prestige by move.
9. Need to integrate planning of both departments, especially budget.
10. P.R. department presently hires outside writers and buys

outside material for magazines. Could use underemployed publicity writers for that.

11. Could save money by phasing out photo lab.

12. Plenty of room in P.R. department offices for moving in publicity personnel. Other departments could use extra space.

Go over this list and test each item for relevance, repetition, and completeness. Ask yourself, "Are any of these items irrelevant to my strategy?" You decide that Item 6 is true but irrelevant. (But you might consider this fact when you write up a plan for carrying out the change.) Is anything repetitive? You notice that 3 and 4 are essentially the same, so you combine them. Do you have enough facts? Is anything skimpy? You know what information you have on hand or will have coming in, but will this be enough? For example, what specific functions of the publicity department are duplicated by the P.R. department? Next, do any of the items have anything in common? For example, items related to saving money, either directly or indirectly, should be grouped together in your outline.

After some scratching out, arrow-drawing to indicate rearrangements of material, and notes to yourself in the margin where more information is needed, you come up with an outline that looks like this:

Introduction: Statement of problem and statement of purpose (brief and general).

Part I   Why the two departments should be merged

    A. Historical reasons for two departments and why these reasons no longer apply.

    B. Both departments would benefit from integrated planning.

       1. Examples of inefficiency and duplication of effort.

       2. P.R. people would benefit from technical skills of publicity people. Give examples.

    C. The company would save money by merging the two departments. Conservative estimate: \$_____.

       1. Photo lab in publicity department could be phased out; pictures processed outside.

2. Underemployed writers in publicity department could take over writing jobs in P.R. department presently farmed out.
3. Extra space in P.R. department could be taken by transferred publicity personnel, thereby freeing _____ square feet for use by _____.

Part II How merger should take place

A. Convince both departments of advantages as outlined in Part I—from their points of view (e.g., moving would give publicity people more prestigious offices; money saved could go into salaries).
B. Make present head of publicity department, assistant director of P.R., other goodies to soften move, make it seem other than a demotion.
C. Involve people in both departments in details of planning physical move.
D. Write new job descriptions for transferred personnel.
E. Have P.R. dept. head work out details of photo lab phaseout.
F. Set a date for accomplishing all this. (Timetable.)
G. Two weeks after move, hold a feedback session to see how the changes are working out.

This outline does not have a separate section for describing the problem in detail. This is done briefly in your introduction because each section of your outline breaks down the problem into its components and states the problems at the same time that it proposes solutions. By doing it this way, you can make your report much shorter. If you devoted space at the beginning to a description of the problems, you'd have to repeat it when you came to your solutions.

Now is the time to put your outline to work to spot weaknesses in your report. The blanks in the outline indicate gaps in your information that must be filled in. In order to come up with a convincing dollar amount saved, you will need to gather more facts under Part I, sections C1, 2, and 3.

Don't worry if your outline still seems sketchy. Smaller

details can always be filled in later, so long as the main divisions are blocked out. If any good ideas for openings or conclusions come to you, jot them down. Give yourself a breather before writing the first draft. Go home, relax, forget it for awhile.

WRITING THE FIRST DRAFT

A story, perhaps apocryphal, is told about a writer who used to put together the first draft of an article by clipping his notes to a clothesline that was strung across his office. He would then stride up and down, reading. When he came to a note that seemed like a good opening, he would take it off the line and begin typing. He'd keep on stalking, peering, and typing until he'd used up all his notes. Then he was finished.

This is not a method we can recommend for most managers. An easier way is to key your material to your outline. When you come to a piece of information that goes into section A 1, write A 1 in the margin of your notes. Do this with every separate piece of information, and when you've finished, cut the sections apart and put the material into the same order as your outline. Now you're ready to begin writing.

Try to write the first draft straight through without interruption. If you have done enough preliminary thinking and planning, the first draft should almost write itself. Take advantage of this momentum. You may be tempted to interrupt your train of thought to worry about the grammar of a sentence or the spelling of a word. *Don't.* Circle it in red or make a note to check it later. Have either the dictation or your handwritten first draft rough-typed double spaced. It's difficult to visualize what the finished page will look like if you're working from a handwritten copy.

Don't be afraid to tear into your first draft. It contains nothing sacred. An old editorial maxim states that good writing is not so much written as rewritten.

REVIEWING THE DRAFT

The more time you can allow between the first draft and revision, the more objectivity you'll have when you come to the task of revision. When you finish writing a first draft, you're too close to it to see its faults. The creator part of you is still going to be too fond of its "baby." You don't need him; you need your severest critic.

Before you revise, check to see if you've stated your main point clearly; included enough supporting facts, details, and examples to convince the reader; and arranged your material in a way that leads the reader from one point to another easily and logically. Checking for these will enable you to discover errors of omission.

You'll also want to know if you've been too wordy, repeated yourself, included material that isn't relevant to your main point, or committed errors in sentence structure, grammar, spelling, and punctuation. In revising, you'll also correct these errors of commission.

While both types of errors are important, you'll want to check for errors of omission first. If there are many of these, your draft will need major surgery.

It's very helpful to get another opinion during the intermission between first draft and revision. Ask someone whose judgment you trust to read your first draft. Pick someone who won't try to flatter you. Professional writers depend on editors for this kind of help because they know that they can't always trust their own opinions. If you wrote it, you tend to see whatever you intended to put there. But when someone else reads it, he or she will see what's actually there.

Tell your reader not to bother correcting your spelling or grammar. The main thing you want to know is whether you got your point across. Ask your reader to sum up your main idea in a single sentence. Has he understood your intent? If his statement of your main point differs from your intention, you have a problem. Ask him what led him to believe that *that* was your main point. You may discover something very interesting.

Even though you started out with a main point in mind, and even though you may have stated it explicitly in your introduction, you can sometimes get carried away as you write. By the time you get to the end, you've allowed your reader to forget your main point. (You may even have forgotten it yourself.) Keep your main point in focus, and restate it somewhere in the conclusion.

If you find distracting irrelevant details, omit them or find a way to work them into the main point. For example, let's say you included an anecdote about how the P.R. department hired a press consultant for one of its campaigns when a former newspaper feature editor was working for the publicity department. But you haven't said *why* you were including this anecdote. Relate it to your main point with something to the effect of, "As an example of wasteful duplication of effort," then tell your anecdote. Emphasize the point of this anecdote by concluding, "It's unlikely that something like this could happen if the P.R. and publicity people were working in the same office."

Often in writing a first draft the relationship of the details to your main point will be clear in your head, so you don't spell them out. But these relationships may elude your reader. Frequently, you'll find that you need to be more explicit.

REVISING THE DRAFT

After you've received the help of a reader, you will want to revise your draft systematically, examining the following:

1. The skeleton (structure and method of organization; corresponds to your outline).
2. The flesh (details that flesh out your outline and make it convincing—facts, examples, statistics; presented in sentences organized into paragraphs).
3. The clothing (words you choose to express your ideas, arranged in clear sentence form).

4. The grooming (correct grammar, spelling, punctuation).

Suppose your reader found it necessary to read C of your memo before he could understand B. Your present order is confusing. So, when revising for structure, you move the parts around; B becomes C and vice versa.

Ask your reader if he finds any parts of your first draft less convincing than others. For instance, you may have come up with very little material to back up the point on dollar savings. On the other hand, the benefits to be gained from integrated planning may have turned out to be greater than you'd anticipated. You decide to shift these sections around, placing the strongest material last, in the most important position.

Your reader may not be able to be this explicit in helping you test the soundness of your structure. He may merely say, "I found this hard to follow." You know that something is wrong, but you're not sure what. Here's a technique that may help you find out:

Take your first draft and outline it in detail *without referring to your original outline.* You may find, to your surprise, that what you actually did was not quite what you planned to do. You may be able to spot misplaced or duplicated parts. Shift the parts around, eliminating whatever duplication you find.

The easiest way to rearrange your first draft is with scissors and tape. Cut the paragraphs apart, rearrange them, then tape them up in your revised order on sheets of paper. Discard any excess.

Fleshing It Out

Your reader's comments about weak or unconvincing arguments may show you where you need to flesh out your outline still more. Have you anticipated possible objections by your readers to what you have to say? Do so, and include answers to possible objections whenever possible.

(This is similar to preparing for the question and answer period during an oral presentation.) For example, how do you know that your plan for putting the merger into effect will work? Have you asked any people in those departments for their opinions or objections?

Is your rough draft flabby or thin? It's thin, no matter how long it may be, if it doesn't include enough specific facts, examples, and statistics to support your generalizations. And it's too flabby if it's repetitious, wordy, and contains meaningless generalizations and unsupported opinions. Compare your paragraphs with the following examples. The second example may be lengthier than the first, but it contains no flab. The first example is fat with meaningless generalities:

1. Failures to achieve something also require proper handling. It pays to develop an approach to them that assures they will not affect working efficiency with others. It is, however, advisable to regularly review them in order to discover their true cause so that it can be eliminated.

2. President Carter's energy proposals have received something less than a standing ovation from the financial community. The bond markets have suffered significant price declines, the dollar has been flogged daily, and gold prices have leaped to record highs. Last Friday, as the world awaited the unveiling of the Administration's new programs, the current four-year Treasury note could be purchased to yield 8.82 percent. This morning (Wednesday) its yield had risen to 8.89 percent, reflecting a decline in price of eight-thirty-seconds, or $2.50 per $1,000 of face value. A Swiss franc on Friday cost 60 cents, while today it costs 62 cents. This may not sound like much, but it is a 3.3 percent decline in three trading days. The price of gold went beyond the $300 level for the first time this morning. The London price stands at $303.85 as compared to $287.45 last Friday, a change of nearly 6 percent.

Now, we're not claiming that example 2 will win any literary prizes, but it's an *honest* paragraph, doing what it sets out to do. If your paragraphs are as full of solid, convincing details as that one, then they're probably pretty good ones. If not, resolve to replace the flab with good, solid meat.

In your first draft, your paragraphs will most likely not be as well organized as they could be. You may jump back and forth between two ideas in a single paragraph, or put details that belong in one paragraph into another. During revision, unscramble those mixed-up paragraphs, put together everything that belongs together, and be alert to opportunities to pare down your paragraphs through better organization. Ask yourself constantly, "What's this paragraph supposed to be about?"

Tailoring the Sentences

In a first draft, some thoughts are bound to be expressed in inappropriate or unnecessary words, inevitably the result of poorly constructed sentences. Consider the following sentence, written by an executive in the manufactured housing (trailer) industry: "It is more or less known in the manufactured housing industry that the demand for service is so great that a top-notch serviceman can make a good living as an independent service contractor."

This sentence can be greatly improved by deleting "It is more or less known." It's not only wordy but it gives an impression of indecisiveness. The sentence then becomes, "The demand for service is so great in the manufactured housing industry that a top-notch serviceman can make a good living as an independent service contractor."

The passive voice is always wordy. Compare "It was voted by the board of directors to declare a dividend" with "The board of directors voted to declare a dividend." Save the passive voice for when you really need it, either to avoid specifying the subject or to emphasize the object: "It was decided to reject . . . ," "It has been determined that . . . ," "The ads were placed in a. . . ."

Often a writer will get carried away and pile on modifying phrases until the sentence sinks under their weight: "She was given a book by the manager of the office for the

sole purpose of keeping records of minor expenditures."
All this means is, "The office manager gave her a book to
keep petty cash records." Be alert for opportunities to combine two sentences into one by making one sentence into a
dependent clause: "All these changes were bitterly opposed by the administration. The administration refuses to
admit that cutting capital gains will increase transactions
and offset part of the tax loss." This can be shortened by
replacing "The administration" at the beginning of the
second sentence with "which."

Of course, the wordy sentence is not necessarily a long
sentence, and long sentences are not always wordy. A
wordy sentence of whatever length is one that has words
that aren't earning their keep. Cut them or replace them
with one word. For example, replace "at this point in time"
with "now." Once you start looking for ways to prune extra
words and sentences, it can become a game to see how
much you can leave out without changing your message. In
fact, one challenge is to reduce your first drafts by at least
one-third and see if they aren't greatly improved.

Just as too many complex sentences or any run-on sentences will confuse your reader, too many short, choppy
sentences can be deadly dull. "The company was mismanaged, it went bankrupt" is a run-on sentence. But "The
company was mismanaged. It went bankrupt" is not necessarily the way to fix it. It would be better to vary your
sentences: "The company was mismanaged and it went
bankrupt" or "Mismanaged, the company went bankrupt"
or "The company, which was mismanaged, went bankrupt." Whenever you notice the same sentence pattern appearing over and over, introduce variety to help keep your
reader attentive.

Some sentences, although grammatical, are extremely
sleep-inducing: "These areas should be considered ex-
peditiously because the department may be called upon to
answer public and congressional inquiry with respect
thereto and this may best be handled outside of DEA because of the involvement of the acting chief inspector."
This example of bureaucratese contains language that is

vague, abstract, and pompous, and the rhythm is jerky and stumbling. Try reading your sentences out loud. If, like this one, they are difficult to get through without stumbling and halting, something is wrong.

Reading well-written magazines and books will also help your writing. It will increase your vocabulary and provide an unconscious model. The rhythms of good English sentences will become second nature.

In revising your draft, watch for words that can confuse your reader. Pronouns can be among the worst offenders.

When an engineer writes, "If the chamber is sealed, it will greatly increase the pressure," what does "it" refer to? In this case, nothing, because "it" is functioning as the subject of "will increase." Does the writer mean that sealing the chamber will greatly increase its pressure, in which case "it" refers to chamber? The answer may be obvious if you're an engineer, but not if you're a general reader.

If you were to write, "Sam Jones, our company president, has just hired Tim Johnson as our new computer expert, and he will be down to see you next week," should the reader expect Jones or Johnson?

Putting aside your first draft for a couple of days before you attempt revision will help you to spot errors in word choice. The real estate salesperson who wrote, "Our conversion of forty-eight motel units into condominiums may be the fastest sellout in real estate history" undoubtedly meant only that the units sold quickly. But since "sellout" also means "betrayal," the choice of words made the triumph sound underhanded.

Does your draft contain any technical language or jargon that your readers will not understand? If you're immersed in this language during your workday, you won't even notice it. You'll have to be on your lookout and translate your specialized vocabulary into more general terms. Similarly, does your draft contain words that are too complex for your readers, mystifying them, or too simple, insulting their intelligence?

Finally, if you have the slightest doubt of a word's meaning, check the dictionary. Using a word that sounds right but is used inaccurately will mislead your audience and embarrass you. If you know the meaning but can't think of the right word, try a thesaurus or Theodore Bernstein's *Reverse Dictionary* (see Bibliography).

The Final Polishing

Just as you want to look your best while giving an oral presentation, you want your writing to look its best. It represents *you* to the reader. This means that it must not only look neat (well typed with wide margins), but it must be correctly spelled and punctuated. Whether fairly or unfairly, people tend to judge the worth of a written communication by its spelling and punctuation. If these put your reader off, he tends to dismiss the content of your message.

Often, correct spelling and punctuation make the difference between saying exactly what you mean and saying something else. The sentence "His faith in his opinion is unshaken" describes someone who has unshaken faith in his own opinion. But "His faith, in his opinion, is unshaken" makes the statement that this person's faith (i.e., religious belief) is, in someone's opinion, unshaken.

Commas, colons, and periods are intended to be the equivalents of pauses in speech. Reading your sentences out loud will help you to identify the places where punctuation is necessary. Many style books now advise a more "open" punctuation, using fewer commas than formerly recommended. You don't need a lot of commas, but those that clarify meaning are needed badly.

Correct spelling is often crucial in English, a language rich in homophones (words that sound the same but are spelled differently). You cite the opinion of an authority but choose a site for a new building and look down the sight of a rifle. Your position may be stationary, but you write letters on company stationery. Often, one letter can make all the difference. When in doubt, check your dictionary. In addition to the dictionary, many writers find *20,000 Words* a handy reference. This lists the spelling of 20,000 of the most commonly misspelled words in English.

And a standard college-level dictionary is one of the best all-around reference tools you can keep on your desk: for checking spelling, reviewing the rules of punctuation, finding names of people and places, foreign expressions, forms of address, and other useful information.

Once you've given your revised version of the memo one last check for spelling, grammar and punctuation, you can turn it over to your secretary for a final typing. When it's in your hands for a final proofing, you'll have a right to feel proud of it. Perhaps going through all these steps took a little longer than usual, but the more practice you get, the more efficient and easier it will become.

EXERCISES

1. Have your secretary give you copies of everything you've written during a typical week. Then do the following:

    a. Ask from one to three people to read an example of your writing and write down your main point in a single sentence. Without consulting them, write down what you thought your main point was. (Do this part in writing.) Now compare what your readers said with your intention. Were they the same? If not, try to figure out why. (You can do this part of the exercise orally with your readers.)

    b. Analyze your own writing, asking the following questions: Should this have been written rather than communicated orally? Was the tone and language right for my audience? Were there too many words that were abstract, too general or technical? Words used sloppily that didn't quite mean what I wanted to say? Words with the wrong connotations? (Check the dictionary.)

2. Have your secretary gather a cross section of the writing done by the people who report to you and subject it to

the same kind of analysis. Do you find any problems with their writing? What will you do about it?

3. Save examples of bad writing that cross your desk. Read them onto a tape recorder, then revise and read your revision onto the tape. Play both versions back. Read a paragraph or two from a well-written business article onto the tape and listen. Can you hear the differences? Bad examples are difficult to read out loud, whereas good examples sound good.

Read a section of a first draft you've written onto a tape recorder. Revise it, then read your revision onto the tape. Play both versions back. Notice any improvement? Do you like what you hear?

4. Reduce your last one-and-a-half or two-page memo to less than one page without losing anything important.

5. If structuring your writing is difficult, try this professional trick: Every time you read a well-written business magazine article, outline it in detail, noting the order, arrangement of material, types of details used, and how they're organized. Use any especially good examples as models.

6. Revision practice: Find one of your reports or memos that you're dissatisfied with. Outline it in detail, then make a new outline to restructure it. Examine some of your own writing for examples of scrambled paragraphs and unscramble them. Also look for examples of wordy sentences and rewrite them.

Bibliography

When all is said and done, we hope that *Communicating Effectively* will aid you in the process of becoming—becoming a better manager, worker, parent; becoming a more knowledgeable person; becoming a more humane and feeling person. Whatever it is that you are in the process of becoming, being a better communicator will help you to accomplish it. This book is a "living" piece, a collection of skills for living that, whether kept at your office for quick reference or next to your bed for late night reading, will provide guidance for whatever task is at hand.

Other books, too, can help you hone your skills and sharpen your insights.

Applebaum, Ronald, et al. *The Process of Group Communications.* Chicago: Science Research Associates, 1974.

Argyris, Chris. *Integrating the Individual and the Organization.* New York: John Wiley & Sons, 1964.

Barnlund, Dean. *Interpersonal Communication.* Boston: Houghton Mifflin, 1968.

Beardsley, Monroe. *Thinking Straight: Principles of Reasoning for Readers and Writers*. 4th ed. Englewood Cliffs: Prentice-Hall, 1975.

Berne, Eric. *Games People Play*. New York: Ballantine, 1978.

———. *What Do You Say After You Say Hello?* New York: Bantam, 1975.

Bernstein, Theodore M. *Bernstein's Reverse Dictionary*. New York: Times Books, 1975.

———. *The Careful Writer: A Modern Guide to English Usage*. New York: Atheneum, 1965.

———. *Do's, Don'ts and Maybes of English Usage*. New York: Times Books, 1977.

Bion, W. R. *Experience in Groups*. New York: Basic Books, 1961.

Birdwhistell, Ray L. *Kinesics and Context: Essays on Body Motion Communication*. Philadelphia: University of Pennsylvania Press, 1970.

Bolles, Richard. *What Color Is Your Parachute?* Berkeley: Ten Speed Press, 1979.

Bormann, E. G. *Discussion and Group Methods*. New York: Harper & Row, 1969.

Burke, Kenneth. *Language as Symbolic Action*. Berkeley: University of California Press, 1973.

Cartwright, Worwin, and Alvin Zander. *Group Dynamics*. New York: Harper & Row, 1968.

Chase, Stuart. *Guide to Straight Thinking with Thirteen Common Fallacies*. New York: Harper & Row, 1956.

Clevenger, Theodore, and Jack Matthews. *The Speech Communication Process*. Chicago: Scott, Foresman, 1971.

Corriere, Richard, and Joseph Hart. *The Dream Makers*. New York: Bantam Books, 1978.

Davis, Flora. *Inside Intuition*. New York: McGraw-Hill, 1971.

Duncan, Hugh Dalziel. *Symbols in Society*. New York: Oxford University Press, 1968.

Dunsing, Richard J. "You and I have Simply Got to Stop Meeting This Way," *Supervisory Management*, November 1979.

Ekman, P., and W. Friesen. *Unmasking the Face*. Englewood Cliffs, N.J.: Prentice-Hall, 1975.

Fast, Julius. *Body Language*. New York: M. Evans & Co., 1970.

———. *The Body Language of Sex, Power and Agression*. New York: M. Evans & Co., 1977.

———. "Face Language: How to Read It," *Family Circle*, July 7, 1979.

Fear, Richard. *The Evaluation Interview*, rev. 2nd ed. New York: McGraw-Hill, 1978.

Flesch, Rudolph. *The Art of Clear Thinking.* New York: Harper & Row, 1951.

———. *The Art of Plain Talk.* New York: Macmillan, 1962.

———. *The Art of Readable Writing.* New York: Macmillan, 1962.

———. *Say What You Mean.* New York: Harper & Row, 1972.

Follett, Wilson. *Modern American Usage.* New York: Warner Books, 1974.

Fowler, H. W. *Modern English Usage.* Ernest Gowers, ed. 2nd ed. New York: Oxford University Press, 1965.

Goffman, Erving. *The Presentation of Self in Everyday Life.* New York: Anchor Books, 1959.

Goleman, Daniel. "People Who Read People," *Psychology Today,* July 1979.

Hall, E. T. *The Hidden Dimension.* Garden City, N.Y.: Doubleday, 1966.

———. *The Silent Language.* Garden City, N.Y.: Doubleday, 1959.

Hayakawa, S. T., et al. *Language in Thought and Action.* 4th ed. New York: Harcourt Brace Jovanovich, 1978.

Hersey, Paul, and Kenneth Blanchard. *Management of Organizational Behavior.* Englewood Cliffs, N.J.: Prentice-Hall, 1972.

Homans, George C. *The Human Group.* New York: Harcourt, Brace, Jovanovich, 1950.

Jay, Antony. "How to Run a Meeting," *Harvard Business Review,* March–April 1976.

Kepner, Charles H., and Benjamin B. Tregoe. *The Rational Manager.* New York: McGraw-Hill, 1955.

Koehler, Jerry, et al. *Organizational Communication: Behavioral Perspectives.* New York: Holt, Rinehart & Winston, 1976.

Korda, Michael. *Power: How to Get It, How to Use It.* New York: Random House, 1975.

Lewis, Norman. *Word Power Made Easy.* New York: Pocket Books, 1953.

Likert, Rensis. *New Patterns of Management.* New York: McGraw-Hill, 1961.

Maier, Norman, and John J. Hayes. *Creative Management.* New York: John Wiley & Sons, 1967.

Maslow, Abraham H. *Motivation and Personality.* New York: Harper & Row, 1954.

Matz, Maxwell. *Live and Be Free Through Psycho-cybernetics.* Warner, 1978.

McClelland, David C., et al. *The Achieving Society.* New York: D. Van Nostrand, 1961.

McGregor, Douglas. *The Human Side of Enterprise.* New York: McGraw-Hill, 1960.

Mehrabian, Albert. *Nonverbal Communication.* Chicago: Aldine, 1972.

——. *Public Places and Private Spaces: The Psychology of Work, Play and Living Environments.* New York: Basic Books, 1976.

——. *Silent Messages.* Belmont, Calif.: Wadsworth, 1971.

Mintzberg, Henry. "Planning on the Right Side and Managing on the Left," *Harvard Business Review,* July–August 1976.

Molloy, John. *Dress for Success.* New York: Peter H. Wyden, 1975.

——. *The Woman's Dress for Success Book.* Chicago: Follett, 1977.

Montague, Ashley. *Touching: The Human Significance of Skin.* 2nd ed. New York: Columbia University Press, 1971.

Morris, Desmond, et al. *Gestures: Their Origins and Distribution.* Stein & Day, 1979.

New York Times Guide to Reference Materials, Mona McCormick, ed. New York: Popular Library, 1971.

Powell, John. *Why Am I Afraid to Tell You Who I Am?* Niles, Ill.: Argus Communications, 1969.

Renwick, Patricia A., and Edward Lawler, et al. "What You Really Want from Your Job," *Psychology Today.* May 1978.

Rivers, William L. *Finding Facts.* Englewood Cliffs, N.J.: Prentice-Hall, 1975.

——. *Writing: Craft and Art.* Englewood Cliffs, N.J.: Prentice-Hall, 1975.

Schein, Edgar H. *Organizational Psychology.* Englewood Cliffs, N.J.: Prentice-Hall, 1965.

Scott, Ian, and Max Luscher, eds. *The Luscher Color Test.* New York: Simon and Schuster, 1969.

Sheehy, Gail. *Passages.* New York: Dutton, 1976.

Shepherd, Clovis R. *Small Groups: Some Sociological Perspectives.* New York: Chandler, 1964.

Siegman, Aron W., and Stanley Feldstein, eds. *Nonverbal Behavior and Communication.* Hillsdale, N.J.: Lawrence Erlbaum Associates, 1978.

Sommer, Robert. *Personal Space: The Behavioral Basis of Design.* Englewood Cliffs, N.J.: Prentice-Hall, 1969.

———. *Tight Spaces: Hard Architecture and How to Humanize It.* Englewood Cliffs, N.J.: Prentice-Hall, 1974.

Stewart, John. *Bridges Not Walls.* Reading, Mass.: Addison-Wesley, 1973.

Strunk, William, Jr., and E. B. White. *The Elements of Style.* New York: Macmillan, 1957.

United Press International Stylebook, Bobby Ray Miller, ed. UPI, 1977.

Yankelovich, Daniel. "The New Psychological Contracts at Work," *Psychology Today,* May 1978.

Zelko, Harold P. *The Business Conference.* New York: McGraw-Hill, 1969.

Index